NOT GHOSTS, BUT SPIRITS

VOLUME II

Querencia Press, LLC
Chicago Illinois

QUERENCIA PRESS

© Copyright 2023
Querencia Press

All Rights Reserved

No reproduction, copy or transmission of this publication may be made without written permission. No paragraph of this publication may be reproduced, copied or transmitted save with the written permission of the author.

Any person who commits any unauthorized act in relation to this publication may be liable to criminal prosecution and civil claims for damages.

ISBN 978 1 959118 43 5

www.querenciapress.com

First Published in 2023

Querencia Press, LLC
Chicago IL

Printed & Bound in the United States of America

CONTENTS

my body is not revolutionary – Alexandria Piette 11
the purge – Alexandria Piette 12
compulsory – Alexandria Piette 14
Untitled – jomé rain 16
Love at the End of the World – Marina Carreira 20
"Sometimes holding on does more damage than letting go" – Marina Carreira 21
Sonnet in the Wild of June – Marina Carreira 22
Ghost Graffiti – Duna Torres Martín 23
cherries in my hair – dre levant 24
heartlurch – dre levant 24
out.. there – dre levant 24
downwards, here i go – dre levant 25
inwards,,? – dre levant 25
Grasping the Mirage – Christina D. Rodriguez 26
Le Duc – Christina D. Rodriguez 27
Remains – Christina D. Rodriguez 28
Beatitudes of a Lingering Dystopia – Christina D. Rodriguez 29
Prize: Fat Girl – Christina D. Rodriguez 30
PMDD—The Insatiable Monster That Won't Stop Chasing Me – Jess Gregory 31
He Or She And Never Us Together – Amelie Honeysuckle 36
In A Trance – Amelie Honeysuckle 37
Stop the World – Dia VanGunten & Beppi 38
medusa. – Paris Woodward-Ganz 46
Gravediggers Lament – Paris Woodward-Ganz 47
Phobics in the World – Revika Sangamita 48
Changing Pronouns: A Step – Revika Sangamita 49
Ace – Revika Sangamita 50
Imagine Girls At Parties – Sara Wiser 51
Kriah: The Mourning – Sara Wiser 53
Untitled – Rachel Coyne 55
Untitled – Rachel Coyne 56
invader – Antonia Rachel Ward 57
mannequin or; the girl with the enamel eyes – Antonia Rachel Ward 58

this is a happy house – Antonia Rachel Ward 59
starlight – Antonia Rachel Ward 60
Girl on a Sidewalk//Boys in a Car – Michele Zimmerman 61
A Right – Heather Meatherall 65
On Being a Woman in STEM – Heather Meatherall 66
Funeral Party – Claire Thom 67
Something Up My Sleeve – Claire Thom 68
Grasp – Sarah Ray 69
I spent a week believing – Sarah Ray 71
I Know Nothing About Being Alive – Sarah Ray 72
Misfired Synapses – Sarah Ray 74
A Moment of Omens – Julie Lee 75
Her Mother's Daughter – Veronica Szymankiewicz 76
Witches – Veronica Szymankiewicz 77
Holy Animal – Mimi Flood 79
Happy Birthday To Me – Mimi Flood 79
Pop Goes the Weasel – Mimi Flood 79
The Slide Down the Highway – Mimi Flood 80
16 – Mimi Flood 81
My Sisters – Kamilah Mercedes Valentín Díaz 82
Cotización – Kamilah Mercedes Valentín Díaz 83
Ballet of the Forget-Me-Nots – S. Kavi 84
Young & Green – S. Kavi 84
Lady Monarch – S. Kavi 85
Blossom – S. Kavi 85
Reunited – S. Kavi 85
Pet the lion – Sarah Merrifield 86
Obituary – Sarah Merrifield 87
i killed the cis girl i was – Roya Motazedian 88
Certain Lines – Rachel Mulder 90
Cowardly Messages – Rachel Mulder 90
Sisterly Glaces – Rachel Mulder 90
Your Mirror is Here – Rachel Mulder 91
To Be Held – Rachel Mulder 91

a poem about the flight & fight to win the right to vote for women :: on suffrage, seeds, & stuff – Jen Schneider 92
To Tell or Not to Tell / At the Intersection of Motherhood and Creativity an elegy (re)framed & (re)plated as "i'm sorry" 99
Your Amazon Fresh Order is Out for Delivery – Jen Schneider 103
Red pin / Jaw wing – Sam Moe 105
NYE – Sam Moe 107
Places They Never Belonged – Mattie-Bretton Hughes 111
Womb – Mattie-Bretton Hughes 112
Once Upon A Time – Mattie-Bretton Hughes 113
A study on (A)sexuality – Dani Solace 116
Doppelgänger: Reflecting on Femininity – Dani Solace 117
why don't I like it? – Dani Solace 117
Pocket Universe – Jenny Benjamin 118
Late Summer – Jenny Benjamin 122
Trans Colors – Jenny Benjamin 123
This or This? – Jenny Benjamin 124
Dissolving Mothers – Ryan Jafar Artes 125
I Watch the Roots – Ryan Jafar Artes 126
Sacrifice – Ryan Jafar Artes 128
(A) Female Parent / (Birth) Mother / (Adoptive) Mother / Mother (?) / Mama / Momma / Amma / Mommy / Mom / Ma – Ryan Jafar Artes 130
The Girl Is Only Allowed to Have One Story – Ryan Jafar Artes 133
Cereals – Culkeeen 134
artifice: a man-constructed thing – Colette Thalia-Rose Stergios 135
in manner hands – Colette Thalia-Rose Stergios 136
hormones – Colette Thalia-Rose Stergios 137
Tears of the Water – Sam Indigo Lydia Fern 138
Vessel – Sam Indigo Lydia Fern 144
The B Isn't Silent – Emily Long 146
Eleven truths and a lie – Emily Long 148
When my friend asks me how I know (I'm queer) – Emily Long 149
A Catalog of Gender Euphoria – Emily Long 150
JoJo Lamboy – AJ Schnettler 151
Androgyny King – AJ Schnettler 152
Dei Garcia – AJ Schnettler 153

you+me as angel numbers – nat raum 154
Non-Binary Switch – Violeta Garza 155
Equator – Violeta Garza 156
Future Vigil for a Generational Wound – Violeta Garza 157
Star-Crossed – Marisa Silva-Dunbar 158
Tempus Aquarius – Stephen Brown 159
Mouse Jail – Stephen Brown 160
My Sister Eats the World – Stephen Brown 161
Red Dress – Veronica S. 162
Untitled – Victoria Johnson 171
On Church Grounds – Isabelle Quilty 172
Star Fire Rising – Madalyn R. Lovejoy 173
A Queer Memory – Madalyn R. Lovejoy 174
Of Critical Cat Calls – Madalyn R. Lovejoy 175
Tuesdays with the Ghost – LindaAnn LoSchiavo 176
I am here – Lee Martínez Soto 178
Dear Cis People: – Lee Martínez Soto 182
All Women Are a Mother's Daughter – Lucy Puopolo 185
doll – Abigail Guidry 187
enough – Abigail Guidry 187
performance – Abigail Guidry 188
scratch – Abigail Guidry 188
The Burden of Blood – Shelley Sanders-Gregg 189
One Day – Tori Louise 190
Imaginary – Tori Louise 193
Object(ive) – Tori Louise 195
the hidden weapon – Lindsay Valentin 197
we made us – Lindsay Valentin 198
the pulp of oneself – Lindsay Valentin 199
Yesterday's sacrarium – Theresa K. Jakobsen 200
Furor Uterinus – Sarah Blakely 201
Ask Me What I Like – Sarah Blakely 202
The Self-Proclaimed Nice Guy – Sarah Blakely 203
Abortion Should Not Be A Synonym For Danger – Sarah Blakely 204
Girls Gone Feral – Sarah Blakely 205

hallowed winter – Lilith Kerr 206
Talk me down – Lilith Kerr 207
unconditional – Lilith Kerr 208
Unapologetically Woman – Brooke Gerbers 209
Take Me out of My Skin – Brooke Gerbers 210
Among the Unlikeable Parts – Brooke Gerbers 211
Before You Say Yes – Brooke Gerbers 212
Good woman – Brooke Gerbers 213
Bonfire night. – Tara Dudhill 215
Before – Julie Elefante 216
Language – Julie Elefante 217
Empty, Full – Julie Elefante 219
Mother Redefined – Julie Elefante 221
Touch Me – Mo McMasters 223
Stone Heart – Korbyn McKale 224
Garden/Body/Prison – Korbyn McKale 225
After I Forgot to Check Under the Bed, ... 226
I Found We Are All Monsters – Korbyn McKale 226
Trapped Butterfly – K.G. Munro 227
Leslie and Rebecca – Moriah Katz 228
Breathe – Dawn Wing 233
MY land – Ananiah J 234
I'm sorry I ruined your wedding – Ananiah J 235
Hold her – Ananiah J 236
yearned, waited, & prayed – Linda M. Crate 237
miracle and magic exist – Linda M. Crate 238
Gusher – Melissa Frederick 239
Ceres – Melissa Frederick 240
The Bluest Lie – Melissa Frederick 241
your feminism – Marianna Pizzini Mankle 242
Not Your Villains – Che Flory 243
Aces Wild Blackberries – Jillian Calahan 246
I Am A Woman – Jillian Calahan 247
Wounded – Annie McCormick 250
Cage – Annie McCormick 250

Word Problems – L.M. Cole 251
1912 – DC Diamondopolous 252
1957 – DC Diamondopolous 255
There Was No Aslan In My Closet – Beni Tobin 258
Do You Believe in Fairies? – Beni Tobin 259
my body's messenger – Haven Rittershofer-Ongoco 260
bloom where planted– Haven Rittershofer-Ongoco 265
collective dreaming – Haven Rittershofer-Ongoco 266
what makes a person non-binary? – riel fuqua 267
sappho's time– riel fuqua 269
Subliminal – Jean Woodleigh 271
Bloody White Veil – Nazmi Shaikh 272
La Llorona – Daniella Navarro 273
poltergeist – Daniella Navarro 274
I Choose What Grows Here – Chelsey Hudson 275
an awakening – Kayla Porth 276
capsule – Kayla Porth 277
a history – Kayla Porth 278
rebirth – Kayla Porth 279
Tread Lightly – Alice Carroll 280

ABOUT THE CONTRIBUTORS 281
OTHER TITLES FROM QUERENCIA 289

my body is not revolutionary – Alexandria Piette (she/her/they/them)

my body is not revolutionary
in the way nature is not rioting,
only threaded through this world
like sweet alyssum woven
around the crown of a head,
a relic of your place in this kingdom.
drinking in early summer feels akin to
the mechanics of lungs;
inhale robins darting across cornflower skies;
exhale the remaining dandelions
we labor to rid the soil of.
as if these weeds are not nourishment,
as if we are not twisting them from their roots
because someone once proclaimed
they are lackluster,
those weeds,
their bodies are treacherous.
nature does not anger from this,
does not act as a renegade
to remind them otherwise.
instead, the dandelions still blossom in clockwork,
the ryegrass like butterscotch
as the sun dips below the treetops
like a weary mother longing for sleep.
i look out into this world like an explorer,
only told where i am to fit,
as though everywhere does not call for me.
instead of fury in the face of this,
i am nature;
i am here,
like dandelions every may,
like lake michigan warmed by aching heat,
and i am endless
in the waves environing me of those
who have been dug up from the earth.

the purge – Alexandria Piette (she/her/they/them)

my body is an ark;
a sailing through a cosmic flood,
divine intervention in a cleansing sea.
on this are my feet,
which carry me through valleys,
grasshoppers and monarch butterflies
fluttering around my blistered soles to guide me,
the friction of chirps and kisses of wings
to remind me that
just beyond the bend,
salvation is close enough that i can just
barely wrap a hand around it—
on this are my hands,
calloused with torn knuckles,
gently holding a cheek,
turning doorknobs,
and kneading my weary eyes—
on this are my eyes,
weathered by the erosion of
everything i should not have witnessed.
my therapist informs me that
this whiplash into days gone by is flashbacks,
and my stomach tumbles forward—
on this is my stomach,
this conflicting anatomy
that i yearn to saw off,
flesh and muscle in a bucket
on the floorboards.
i have learned to love this stomach—

this body and brain
that which synapses form supernovas
beneath the surface of skin.
this water,
this torrent—
it cannot purify me when
i am the temple at which i pray.
still,
it will purge this humanity of its blasphemy,
for ever persuading me that i was
condemned for my size;
for the forty days and forty nights
i devoted to loathing;
for the vomit i masqueraded as penance.
let the ocean swallow them whole,
i command.
let them see me liberated on this holy ark.

compulsory – Alexandria Piette (she/her/they/them)

i've lost myself
beneath the bellies of men,
and therein lies a part of me
that wishes i hadn't.
dreaming on a shooting star
is futile when your bones
have already been encompassed
by the ravenous hunger of the
shadows;
your body alive in its stomach,
digesting.
the truth is,
where i exist now—
i see women,
and suddenly,
my fragmented, dying lightbulb
plucks itself out of the waste,
and glues itself back together inside of me.
i used to think that falling in love with a man
was something that i couldn't control.
and i *couldn't*;
i have loved men,
but not in the way i have loved women.
i reflect on myself at thirteen,
scrolling through
the burgeoning abyss of media,
and how i witnessed couples,
but i never witnessed something happy.
everything was always
decaying.

and then,
slowly,
but with grace,
i acknowledged that within me,
there was something
so pigmented in color and hue—
this scintillating, rainbow lens—
that i could never let it go.
and i haven't.
i asked her, "would you still love me if i liked boys and girls?"
and then, "i love women."
and nothing changed.

Untitled – jomé rain (she/her)

Tell me, angel—are you angry at the earth or the drywall that stands upon its surface?

Either way, fists are raised. No matter the direction, you keep punching.

****

In the dream where the brown fingered man cruises down the coastline and I am riding shotgun, a bear appears on the road, and I think of another love who tried to lead me to the forest, and how I always lost my way.

In this dream, there are no traffic laws, and so the brown fingered man places both glowing hands around my face and stares at me from the glove compartment, like dismembered eyes of Sauron. His palms cover my whole mask so that I may be free to remove it, but I do not bite, I push my disguise further into his warmth until the two are blending, until my simulacrum begins to melt into his truth and he wails, retracting his hands as I cough up bloody sand onto the dashboard.

He looks down into his honey hands, already healing around the scorched imprints of my resistance.

"I still haven't found a decent use for them."

I sweep the muddy red sand out of the window, out of our way, and it trails behind us as we speed down the road, a shooting star, a chemtrail.

The bear is late and the script is wrong.

"I still haven't found a decent use for you," he sighs, pulling over.

The graveyard is empty and warm. I think of the dead, my sweet Honey Hands, et l'ours qui m'a posé le lapin. How did we get here? Where are we going?

Let us not confuse what we do with who we are, okay? You're still good, you're still good, close your eyes, you are still *good.*

Speak up, little one. You/we are an embryo, a chrysalis, a bold growing star beam floating through space, ready to jump into a tesseract in spite of all better judgement. You/we wanted to be useful and so devoured, little monster. Look what you've done to our sweet Honey Hands. You didn't mean to do it. You're still good, you're still golden, he's still buried, you're still good.

Choose a perspective. Are you the victim or the witch? This is not the time to phone a friend, there are no lifelines here. Pick a side. Princess or poison? There are no wrong answers, there are only his hands, and a gravesite, a hollow space built for one that demands an offering, if only you'd choose your role. Are we corpse or executioner? Do you want to flip a coin?

****

Hell is a place that feels like a hug. Hell is a place so familiar.

My little bird body is shivering within the cold comfort of the air conditioning which blasts full force on this rainy, sunken day.

Do not get too comfortable, she whirrs.
Still, always, there is a job to be done.

I never thought that hell would be so frigid. I imagined sticky hot springs, debauchery and open sores, demons licking my wounds, something full and molten, my lover's angry magma seething through my cracks.

Come to find that hell is fluorescent lights, relentless sterility, a hospital bed, an odourless locker room. Hell is a shopping mall you can't escape, it's free trials and perfume samples. It is a blonde teenager shoving lip plumpers down her waistband and the security guards who are too exhausted to unionise, let alone protest.

Hell becomes you, becomes us. If we were made in god's image, then hell was built in our honour, a bespoke love letter that we all take turns signing and cosigning until the postman ceases collection. Hell becomes the leopard print blanket that you curl up within, hell becomes the black box of moving image we pore into like lobotomised infants, hell becomes the distance between us, between calls, hell becomes saline, though it was never meant to be so wet here.

Hell is backspace and forwards, infinitely looping through words that don't fit, that suffocate you in the space that they could never fill. I hide behind 'you'. I speak to 'you' in lieu of speaking to 'me', in lieu of speaking to mirrors. One day, I'll have my own house and there will be no mirrors—just hardwood floors and soft jazz, sunshine pouring in through the big bay windows whose glass will be designed to capture everything except reflections. In my big dream home, there will always be fresh fruit, and faeries will play in the garden. Sometimes friends will visit—they'll bring me amber honey and invite me to lick it up off their warm, glowing hands.

****

Last night I dreamt I was trapped in a foster care facility that reminded me of Cable Street.

The cold corridors, spray painted walls that suggested a modicum of privacy that was never truly found, when a room reflects a prison and every moment spent outside is a moment you wish you could return to your cell.

In this dream, I am less docile, I conspire with the other lost children to steal the keys from the warden's daughter, we will escape in the night and we will not return. One of them says so, "they won't let us back in if we leave," and we have to explain to her, *that's the point, exactly.*

In this dream, there is a love affair. There is always a love affair in my dreams, and my co-star tonight is an actor, I know him, or know of him, both from silver screen and other dreams in which he frequently makes an appearance. The details get fuzzy, but the picture remains—his face, a lofty bedroom, the elevator that carries us down but will not pull us up, not if we have anything to say about it, not unless it's lifting our cold, limp corpses.

In the real foster care, the one that feels so distant, like there was another me who took my place and forwarded me the cliff notes of trauma to tap into at a later date—in that building there were no boys, nor allies, just a hollow little girl looking for an elevator and a contraband cellphone that she hid in a cardboard diorama of her dream home, the one she built in art therapy.

Really, her dream home, the home that I have in all my dreams, looks nothing like the picket fenced cellophane model I kept in my cell. The home of my dreams is a loft, an ever-expanding labyrinth of white floors and spiral staircases, hidden doors that lead to pockets of nowhere, or Narnia, and no matter how far we climb, we never reach the top.

There is something to be said here about the subconscious, the shopping mall hellscape, the layers upon layers of philo puff promise.

****

I've been conjuring again, it seems.

I shouldn't have spoken about the dream loft. Whenever we meet, nowadays, it is always in the dream loft. You (the only you, not the 'you' from some pages before, the real you, the one who this is written for)—you have been gone for two years. The last year, I made a promise—I told myself I would not use your name, I would not speak of you, I would not write of you. I swore to wash my mouth of you for one year, and I did. I made it through. Sometimes I would feel you lurch up in my throat and I would swallow you back, my darling bile, I would draw you back to the depths where I left you. My sweet, sweet Honey Hands.

I got cocky. I did not want to speak ill of the dead, and so I stopped speaking of you at all, and I forgot the power your memory possesses, I thought I could talk of the house without thinking of you, the water rocking beneath us—I forgot about my sea legs, I thought I was so steady...

Now you're back, of course. To remind me of the forever distance between myself and the ground beneath me, you like to pop in sometimes, whenever I feel safe—drinking my Lavender Oats, you enter the chat and you make your presence, you make your power known.

I shouldn't have spoken about the Dream House. I should have left you in the grave.

I ask my father what there is to be done when what you've buried crawls up to haunt you. He shakes his head.

Jomé, what have I always told you about that which you kill?
Before you pour the dirt, make sure they're really dead.

So this is my fault, clearly. I didn't want to bash your face in. I didn't want to check your pulse.

Remember when you left yourself behind and tasked me with cleaning up your mess? You never thanked me. You asked me to do it, and then you never thanked me, just nibbled on my bloody fingertips and compared the taste to Malbec. You tell me I wouldn't know the difference between a god and a grape juice if it scaled up my throat, dripped down my chin. You tell me that my original sin was loving you, because you never asked me to, because you actively advised against it.

(I should've made sure you were dead.)

Love at the End of the World – Marina Carreira (she/they)

Let's pack for everywhere tonight;
Make prom of the apocalypse—
scorching dancefield where goats roam

from the dinner table, children bouquet
their grandmothers' bones, widows sing
like sparrows lost at sea—die a little death

with me on this pyre of poppy;
be the pulp people feast on, the marrow
of love staining them in Revelation.

“Sometimes holding on does more damage than letting go” – Marina Carreira (she/they)

Lately, I get my wisdom from internet memes,
direction from the social media gods filling my algorithm
with messages about how trauma bonded us,
how trouble followed us, how torment fills us,
how we’ve tried and tried to stay in the ring and fight
for a life grounded in grief. Man, oh man, have we tried
everything but letting go, and maybe it’s time
to put the gloves away, slide back into our respective corners,
confess our biggest fear: love just ain’t enough.
Let the bell ring. Listen to Facebook posts from divorcees
who claim to be doing bad all by themselves, leave with
whatever good grew in between the cracks.

Sonnet in the Wild of June – Marina Carreira (she/they)

I pretend it's some other month,
some other badland to bad mouth
my shit luck in. Elisabete says *it's all part*
of the universe's plan: the nightmare job,
the relapse, the teething dog: groundhog's days
of regret. Pity—party of one. Still, I demand
better from this beautiful planet: its golden pampas
and crystalline lakes; red rocks and salt flats.
The bodega with the new AC blasting over
the blue Icees. The deranged hydrant spraying
rainbows over hard gravel. This world owes
every queer addict mother their dream deferred:
cake by the ocean, a gown of pills, a baby as safe
as a gun in the hands of an old white man.

Ghost Graffiti – Duna Torres Martín (she/her)

Joint by a shared fear of the
last time we forgot everything, we
tailless angels of snow-covered strolls
ran away from the lights too bright,
rooms too glooming from
the fear of being quite forgotten
& now we bite a spoonful
of rediscovery.

Reawakened, in a cat house, ingenerated from
engendering new meanings, breaking
old rules, the endless graffiti blooms all
over our once neighborhood's palisade
shadowing the whiskers of
survival, the shivering shelter where
the ink turns root,
the alloy turns nightshade,
the gravel,
floret
expanding.

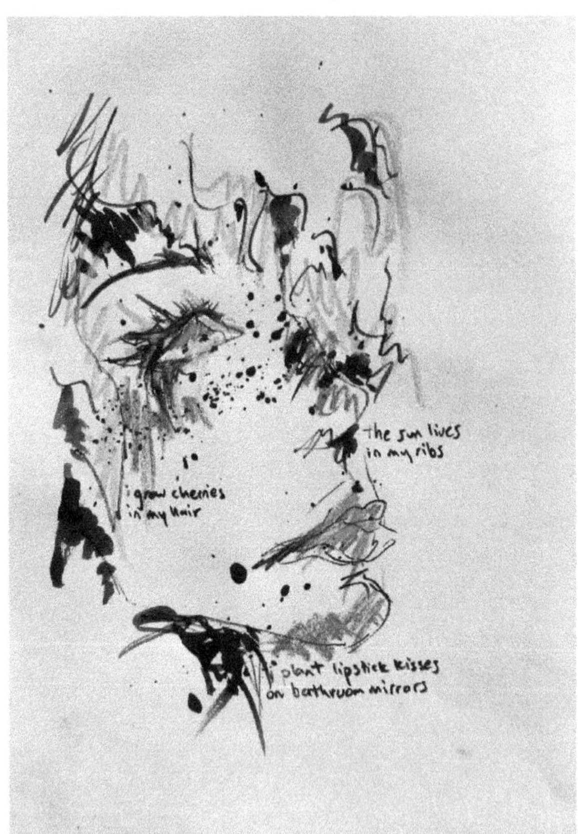

cherries in my hair – dre levant (they/he)

out.. there – dre levant (they/he)

heartlurch – dre levant (they/he)

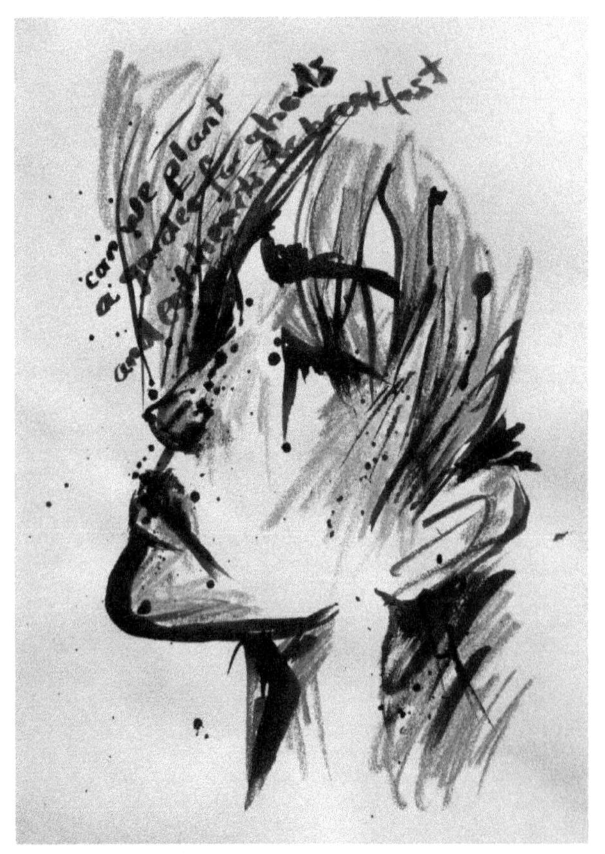

downwards, here i go – dre levant (they/he)

inwards,,? – dre levant (they/he)

Lately I've discovered a new joy in my art—making scribbly and colourful portraits with a mixture of sharpie, crayon, and ink. It's less about creating a polished piece of art and instead creating pieces with intuition and playfulness at the forefront. As someone who is trans masc, having the freedom to express myself in bright colours and outside the lines is very important. All of these pieces are explorations of expression, exploration of art that is fun to make, and art that comes from a place of pure creativity and queer joy.

Grasping the Mirage – Christina D. Rodriguez (she/her)

you grew on the nectar of a mirage,
a study in the rumination of hours as pastime,
a burgeoning bedroom tongue
carrying a constant tether to one another.

i want to be the crown to your instant.
the smirk of the ah-ha of your eyebrows.
the split second to your hull of cravings.
our laughter is currency for butterflies born of refuse.

i want you in a vacuum of uncertainty.
my ego wants your reciprocation, a fool's moon
of benediction as the ink to the Aesop in my head
falling in the vicinity of kindred soft spots.

i want to grasp you in carafes of psalms,
an episode of being dusk of scripture
written in the ego of a wayward woman,
spinning around the fable of a madhouse infatuation.

¿te conjuro la soga de un idioma que solo nosotros entendemos o la soledad de tirar un bolígrafo?

Le Duc – Christina D. Rodriguez (she/her)

We wander
warmly through our
private catacombs.

I inhaled
the night under
the collar
of her dress.

She smiled
a martyr's smile
for her own
benefit

a fire
that solitude
presses
against my lips.

Things left
unspoken,
angels ripped
from wombs—

I walk without
flinching through
the burning
cathedral of
the summer

—the squid in
my guts
shuddered.

Remains – Christina D. Rodriguez (she/her)

On her neck, a sliced bone, a relic of an old god
dangles above her right hand, waiting to be cremated.

The deadweight of their yesteryears arch her towards
submission; she defiantly keeps her knees above water.

I don't want to remember your name, she prays to a former
life, *I only want to be baptized in what remains without a memory.*

Grief forms a body that can never be cindered,
a replacement of every left that hasn't been right.

And a god dwells on in a place that can't be burned.

Beatitudes of a Lingering Dystopia – Christina D. Rodriguez (she/her)

As she made me cry
in the ruins of childhood,
scattered on top
of an ancient television set
—the box filled with 76 winters.

Luckily, those memories floated
back into the clouds,
the basement door swelled
from the storm.

Cherry blossoms arrived
as if on cue,
her diaphragm uncaged.
She'd only remember green
—open-mouthed seed, bearing
a name in the dead
kingdom of Eden.

Prize: Fat Girl – Christina D. Rodriguez (she/her)

Your body is a small-town trophy for the around-the-way boys who didn't get a taste the first time around. In the city that never sleeps with fat girls in public, you're the cocky boys' secret fetish. The ones who know their smile makes you blush, who hold the body of gods, who flex their charm to your quivering knees. They slide into private screens with proposals of covert ecstasy, booking late-night appointments after the buses stop running. They offer their bodies with the arrogance of holy grail, thinking theirs is the only one on your altar.

These are the boys who never tell you, *You're pretty*. They comment on the depth of your throat, the strength of your knees, the dew between your thighs. They never ask *how was your day*, they hardly answer to *how was yours*. They have a sixth sense in knowing when you are over their games and pop up when you are doing just fine. These boys are in it for the chase, to quell a curiosity of *Do big girls do it better? A big girl is a freak.*

They won't be your friend in the light, but they know how to turn on the denial in your body as you attempt to dig for substance and connect. These boys are conquer-bines, looking to feed their egos with a woman they would never be able to keep up with, in a body that matches the depth of her heart. Have her and she's the Plan B on the shelf—an ornament he'll leave with a shallow engraving you'll trace as another notch on the belt you let him slip off.

PMDD—The Insatiable Monster That Won't Stop Chasing Me - Jess Gregory (she/her)

CW: suicidal ideation, self-harm, violence, dissociative episodes, intrusive thoughts, trauma.

I wanted to be able to write this story from a light-hearted perspective.

I wanted to be able to poke fun at myself and all the crazy things I've said and done. In fact, I was originally going to use the title: *Craving Violence? You Could Have PMDD!*

I wanted to be able to laugh at the fact that this sweet, softly spoken girl from a sunny, laid-back town in Australia was the unlikely vessel for the violent beast that is this condition; but in reality, there is nothing funny about what I, or millions of other PMDD sufferers go through.

15 years ago, life was going pretty much as I had hoped. I had just started high school, was doing well in my classes, making new friends, and was recognised as a kind, gentle and charitable person—the one that everyone came to for support and advice. I was by no means a perfect angel, but I think it's important to understand my character in order to appreciate the shock value of what happened next.

I started to have episodes of severe anxiety, everyday tasks started to feel overwhelming. I also experienced long stretches where I seemingly lost the ability to get along with *anyone* in my life. I started to interpret casual comments as personal attacks. What's more, I could barely control my anger in response to these perceived slights. I would come home from school only to scream and hit my pillow, or even myself, in order to release the tension of holding in this ferocious rage.

A year later, I started seeing a psychologist. She didn't seem to think it was unreasonable that I was having profound anxiety. It had been a rough year. I had started experiencing chronic pain, repeated hip and shoulder dislocations, and family illness. I was also dealing with bullying and harassment both in person and online because of my good grades and gentle demeanour.

We worked on some techniques to manage depression and anxiety. It was helpful to have an objective person to talk to about the challenges I was facing, but I didn't really feel like I was making much practical progress. What's more, my mental health was going through long peaks and troughs that didn't seem to correlate to the events happening in my life.

In upper high school, things took a dark turn. My anxiety and anger problems were even further heightened. I began acting them out by harming myself or hitting things around me. I would have dissociative episodes where I would become so submerged in a negative memory that I would speak out loud about what I was seeing without realising it. Frighteningly, when I regained conscious thought, I would sometimes realise that I had broken something around me. It started with small things like pens and pencils, and eventually progressed to bigger objects like coat-hangers and glasses. Sometimes I would find teeth marks or bruises on my arms or realise that I had pulled some of my hair out.

I started to become paranoid and weighed down by a constant sense of danger. I feared talking to people, walking outside, and sometimes just getting out of bed. I also started having intrusive thoughts about causing more serious harm to myself or others. My dissociative episodes became even more severe; sometimes I would perceive that I was being spoken to by someone who wasn't there, usually a particular person that was linked with a (true) traumatic memory.

During the period in which my symptoms were escalating, my mum had already started to talk to me about Pre-Menstrual Syndrome (PMS) and how she felt that my out of character behaviour was coinciding with two weeks out of the month.

She also told me that at the age of 4 (!) I had two episodes of menstrual bleeding which were later attributed to Autonomous Functioning Cysts. A few days before these episodes, she had noticed a significant change in my temperament; I was transforming overnight from a relatively easy-going child, to one that was highly irritable and quick to anger.

She said that what was happening now was reminiscent of those sudden changes, and that it had been worse since I had started using a particular contraceptive pill for Menorrhagia (a common disorder which causes medically significant menstrual bleeding).

Looking back, what she was saying should have been revelatory to me, but at the time, I was simply not in my right mind and was unable to recognise the importance of what she had observed. I was dealing with other serious, physical health issues by then, and was also frightened of coming off the pill because of the fucking *enormous* blood clots I had been passing without it (up to the size of a post-it note!).

I dabbled in a few of the first line treatments for PMS, such as supplements and contraceptive pills, but it wasn't until the end of my undergraduate degree that I finally had enough sense-of-self to have a frank discussion with my doctor about just how much my menstrual cycle seemed to be affecting me.

I sobbed uncontrollably as I opened up for the first time about the self-harm, intrusive thoughts and the fact that I felt like I was going crazy and didn't seem to be able to cope with "mood swings" normally, like other women did.

Fortunately, my doctor recognised the seriousness of my situation and referred me to a gynaecologist who had experience in treating cases like mine. She was very thorough in taking my medical history and the specifics of exactly how and when these cyclical symptoms were affecting me. She asked me to withdraw from the medications I was using to (barely) keep my symptoms at bay, track my progress, and return to her six months later.

It was the hardest six months of my life. It turned out that using hormonal contraceptives was doing more for me than I thought. Without them, I was plunged into a deep depression. At the time, I was teaching music lessons at a school that I loved, yet I was frequently coming close to crying in the staff room in-between my classes. Additionally, I was scared to go to the train station alone at night after my concerts, because I'd have the urge to jump onto the tracks.

While in retrospect I definitely should not have let this go on for as long as I did, this experiment confirmed two important things:

1. My psychological/psychiatric symptoms were only occurring between ovulation and menstruation (although my mood was often low when I got my period because of what I had been through in the preceding weeks).

and...

2. I was only averaging about 4-6 days a MONTH without uterine or pelvic pain.

What. The. Fuck.

I couldn't believe what my notes were telling me—was my life really this bad? How did I let it get to this stage? How did my *doctors* let it get to this stage!?

I realised I had become a victim of own resilience. Forcing myself to go to school or work year after year as my pain got worse had made it seem insignificant to those around me. Similarly, my desire to not have others worry about me, and therefore downplay by psychiatric symptoms, had lead them to be written off as "regular" PMS.

I was finally diagnosed with Pre-Menstrual Dysphoric Disorder (PMDD) upon returning to the gynaecologist and she immediately loaded me up with information on risks, key symptoms, and how the disorder can be distinguished from PMS—the most important of which was a warning about the associated suicide risk.

Although the exact figures are not known, it's estimated that around 1 in 20 people who menstruate have PMDD, and that 30% of those will attempt suicide at least once.

In regards to their similarities, PMS and PMDD may both share physical symptoms such as bloating, breast tenderness, headaches, fatigue, difficulty concentrating, and sleep disturbances. They both also have the potential to cause psychological symptoms such as depression, anxiety, irritability, and a sense of overwhelm.

PMDD is specifically defined as when these symptoms occur with severity (particularly in regards to reactivity and irritability) and significantly impair a person's ability to lead a normal social, personal, or professional life. In extreme cases, PMDD also has the capacity to cause psychosis, paranoia, and dissociation.

Unsurprising, I later learnt that it's very common for PMDD sufferers to be misdiagnosed with Bipolar Disorder, which is why it is *so* important take note of the second part of the diagnostic criteria: that symptoms must begin 1-2 weeks before menstruation, and resolve within the first few days of bleeding.

Although the exact cause of PMDD is not known, there is emerging research demonstrating that it could be due to either abnormal hormone levels or an abnormal reaction in the brain to the normal hormonal changes that happen after ovulation. Some research also shows that people with pre-menstrual mood disorders have abnormal serotonin neurotransmission with a lower density of serotonin transporter receptors.

My gynaecologist and I decided that the best thing for me to do next would be to try a high progesterone contraceptive, so I had a Nexplanon inserted into arm shortly afterwards.

At first, things seemed to be going really well. The Nexplanon was the first contraceptive to successfully suppress my ovulation, and as a result, I had very few PMDD symptoms. My periods did become quite erratic, but for me, it was a more than worthwhile trade off.

Unfortunately, after about a year, my periods became very heavy and near constant, resulting in my new doctor recommending I have it removed. I was extremely disappointed and scared. Not only had I just moved to a different country, but I was also dealing with a slew of worsening musculoskeletal issues, leaving me completely overwhelmed by my new life.

Fortunately, the new doctor had a good understanding of the potential severity of menstrual health problems and recommended the vaginal ring, as it released much lower dose hormones in a localised way—directly up towards the uterus (the phrase "beam me up Scotty!" sprang to mind at the time, but maybe that's just me). This would be combined with a low dose SNRI (serotonin and norepinephrine reuptake inhibitor).

At first, this was a massive win for me; it not only improved my psychological symptoms in an unprecedented way, but also had the unexpected side effect of greatly reducing my Fibromyalgia pain.

The positive effects of these medications gradually dropped off over the course of about 9 months. While my symptoms are still nowhere near as bad as they once were, I have had to keep gradually increasing my SNRI in order to keep the panic attacks and urge to self-harm at bay. I have also been passing more and more blood clots and experiencing increasing pain in-between periods.

Since starting this new regime, I have also been diagnosed with Ehlers-Danlos Syndrome and have discovered that taking progesterone is known to greatly increase joint laxity, something that negatively affects my pre-existing conditions. Although age and genetics are also likely to blame, my gradual uptick in muscular skeletal problems over the past three years is almost certainly in part due to my unwitting use of the Nexplanon.

Frankly, I feel stuck. High oestrogen pills make me feel depressed, high progesterone pills make all my joints fall out of their sockets, and "intermediate" dose pills and non-hormonal methods don't do enough for my pelvic and uterine pain. I can't tolerate NSAIDS, and don't even get me *started* on all the side effects I have to deal with every time I up my dose of SNRIs.

I often find myself feeling hopeless over my lack of options, and distraught over how health issues that primarily affect women and people of minority genders continue to be downplayed and sidelined.

Unfortunately, there is no happy ending to this story.

For now, all I can do is get up every day and make the choice to keep fighting.

I will never again roll over and accept a life filled with physical and emotional pain or be a victim of our (sometimes) vastly inadequate medical system. I know that I, and everyone else who lives with the added risk and responsibilities of having ovaries, deserve so much more.

Recommended Reading:

MGH Center for Women's Mental Health provides a clear explanation of the distinction between PMS and PMDD. It also explains the need to rule out other psychiatric illnesses which have similar features. It has an excellent summary of potential treatment options and current research into the potential causes of PMDD.

BMC Women's Health presents an in-depth qualitative study into women's experiences going through the diagnostic process for PMDD. It outlines the challenging nature of receiving a diagnosis and finding effective, personalised treatments. It also includes some potentially distressing accounts of the symptoms that some women experienced before diagnosis and the grief they carried after realising how much of their life had been lost to PMDD.

The Independent has an article that uses the personal story of 'Sarah' to highlight some of the more extreme symptoms of PMDD such as psychosis. It also outlines how a lack of education within the medical community has lead to many women receiving improper care or feeling stigmatised.

Mind provides advice on how to be effectively evaluated for PMDD and how to minimise the risk of being misdiagnosed. However, they fail to list some of the symptoms that occur in more extreme cases such as psychosis and paranoia.

The HMSA and The Ehlers-Danlos Society have information for hypermobile/EDS patients on navigating women's health issues and how their treatment needs may vary from the general public.

The International Assocation for Pre-Menstrual Disorders has information on some of the specific issues faced by transgender individuals with PMDD and how the rest of us can be better allies.

He Or She And Never Us Together – Amelie Honeysuckle (she/her)

A croaky voice calls from the stairs that spiral.

"You left without calling,"

"And what is it to you, master? Can I not do what I wish?"

"Independently unsettled."

The gloomy house lays on top of my shoulders,
pushing them down,
even touching the smile I held outside the home,
slicing it down into a frown.

"How is your lover? Does he still wash the dishes?"

"No father, she does not."
I continue on,
lost and unfound.
I wish to go back to my real home,
one that actually glows,
and one I truly know.

"Why are you rarely here? Don't you miss me."

I choke on my soup.
Not because it is boiling hot,
but because of the words that always dominate me,
guilt.
Putrid.
"Would you look at the time! 3:05! An hour here is five years off my life!"

"Always the same."

"I could say the same for you."

In A Trance – Amelie Honeysuckle (she/her)

Blossom and flounder,
I cannot believe I have found her.
Perfect and sexy,
one I could eat and make so very messy.

We twirl in the kitchen.
I kiss her lips without hesitation.
A gallery I have known,
even before we first talked on the phone.

The moment I met you,
I knew it was you,
and with us we will love,
forever unplugged.

Kiss me goodnight,
kiss me good morning.
My one and only,
I cannot wait for you to explore me.

Stop the World – Dia VanGunten (she/her) **& Beppi** (she/her)

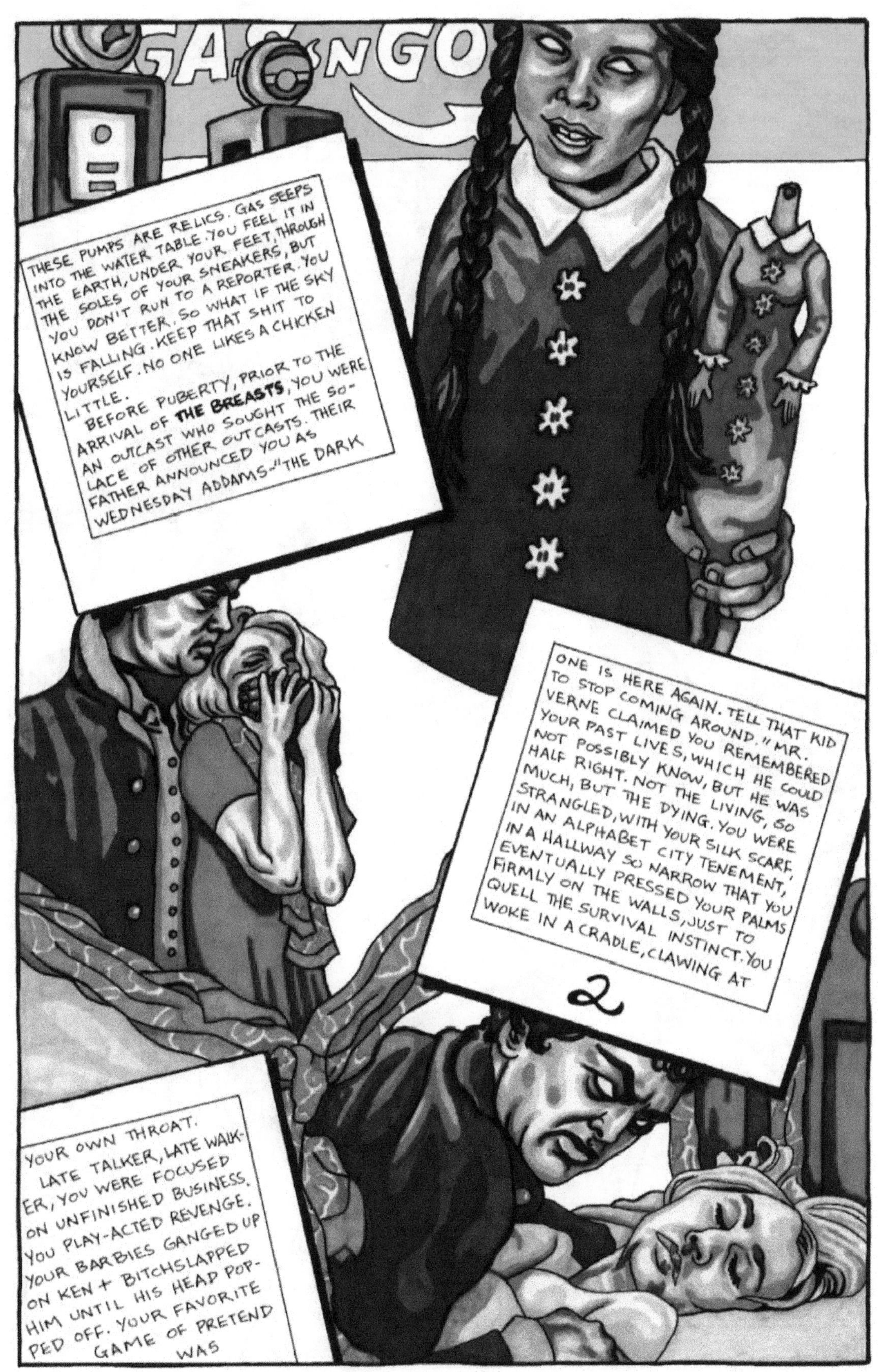
GAS 'N GO
THESE PUMPS ARE RELICS. GAS SEEPS INTO THE WATER TABLE. YOU FEEL IT IN THE EARTH, UNDER YOUR FEET, THROUGH THE SOLES OF YOUR SNEAKERS, BUT YOU DON'T RUN TO A REPORTER. YOU KNOW BETTER. SO WHAT IF THE SKY IS FALLING. KEEP THAT SHIT TO YOURSELF. NO ONE LIKES A CHICKEN LITTLE.
BEFORE PUBERTY, PRIOR TO THE ARRIVAL OF **THE BREASTS**, YOU WERE AN OUTCAST WHO SOUGHT THE SOLACE OF OTHER OUTCASTS. THEIR FATHER ANNOUNCED YOU AS WEDNESDAY ADDAMS-"THE DARK
ONE IS HERE AGAIN. TELL THAT KID TO STOP COMING AROUND." MR. VERNE CLAIMED YOU REMEMBERED YOUR PAST LIVES, WHICH HE COULD NOT POSSIBLY KNOW, BUT HE WAS HALF RIGHT. NOT THE LIVING, SO MUCH, BUT THE DYING. YOU WERE STRANGLED, WITH YOUR SILK SCARF, IN AN ALPHABET CITY TENEMENT, IN A HALLWAY SO NARROW THAT YOU EVENTUALLY PRESSED YOUR PALMS FIRMLY ON THE WALLS, JUST TO QUELL THE SURVIVAL INSTINCT. YOU WOKE IN A CRADLE, CLAWING AT
2
YOUR OWN THROAT.
LATE TALKER, LATE WALKER, YOU WERE FOCUSED ON UNFINISHED BUSINESS. YOU PLAY-ACTED REVENGE. YOUR BARBIES GANGED UP ON KEN + BITCHSLAPPED HIM UNTIL HIS HEAD POPPED OFF. YOUR FAVORITE GAME OF PRETEND WAS

THE MURDER OF SOME LONG DEAD BASTARD FROM THE 40's. ANTONIO NAPOLITANO. YOU LOOKED HIM UP ON MICROFICHE + MISTER MACHISMO WENT OUT LIKE A PUSSY. WHEN A RIVAL GUNNED HIM DOWN IN A BARBER SHOP, HE LOST CONTROL OF HIS BOWELS. THE HEADLINE WAS SHIT N' SHAVE. THE APOS-TROPHE WAS A DOLLOP OF SHAV-ING CREAM. OR MAYBE IT WAS A SWIRLED POO, LIKE THE EMOJI.
BAR
YOUR SUPPRESSED SURVIVAL INSTINCT KICKED IN WITH PUBERTY, WHEN YOU FINALLY REACHED THAT STAGE WHERE KIDS FORGET THEIR LAST REINCARNATION. AMNESIA WAS THE ONLY CHANCE YOU HAD IN THIS LIFE. YOUR SOCIAL STAND-ING IMPROVED. (COULDA BEEN THE TITS. PEOPLE WILL OVERLOOK ALL KINDS OF PERSONALITY MALFUNCTIONS FOR A HEFTY SET OF NATURALS.) BEFORE THE BOOBS, THERE WAS JUST THE ONE FRIEND; TECHNICALLY,
3
FRAN
SAY
RELA
THERE WERE TWO, BUT THE TWINS SHARE AN OPERATING SYSTEM, EVEN NOW, AS GROWN MEN. WHEN YOU STARTED FUCKING THE STRAIGHT ONE, YOU FELT THE OTHER UNDER THEIR SHARED FACE, ALWAYS

MOVING BENEATH THE SKIN OF HIS BROTHER. YOU TRIED TO PULL ATOM TO THE SURFACE BECAUSE YOU WANTED HIM TO KNOW YOUR POWER. (+ ALSO YOU FEEL SAFEST IN THEIR PAIRED PRESENCE.) EVEN NOW, HAPPIER THAN EVER, YOU PLAY THE PRINCESS BRIDE WHENEVER YOU REQUIRE COMFORT.
YOU FEEL JUDGED WHEN NETFLIX ASKS IF YOU'RE STILL WATCHING. YOU TOLD JENNY THAT + SHE SAID, "YAH, MACHINES HAVE LOTS OF THOUGHTS ON US." THE SO-CALLED CONSUMMATE PROFESSIONAL HAS BEEN LETTING THINGS SLIP. THE STRICTURES OF
HER POSITION, OR HER RELIGION, ALL OF THAT IS LOSING RELE-VANCE. IT'S FUN, BUT YOU WONDER IF SHE'S LOST HOPE. OR MAYBE SHE HAS THE VIRUS. NAH. IT'S LOVE, IT'S YOU. YOU FUCKED THE JOB RIGHT OUT OF HER. YOU TRIED TO DO THE SAME TO ATON, TO EXORCISE THE TWIN, BUT IT NEVER TOOK. YOU WASTED YEARS ON HETEROSEXUALITY. THAT THING-"MAN"-WAS MEANINGLESS IN THE END. YOU WERE ONLY ATTRACTED TO MEN BECAUSE OF BIOLOGICAL IMPERATIVE. YOU WERE PRE-
4
Continue
Exit
OCCUPIED WITH THE D, BUT IT'S YOU. YOU ARE THE DICK. ATON WAS THE ONLY PERSON WHO KNEW YOU, + YOU'VE KNOWN HIM FOREVER, BUT ONLY NOW, WITH THIS SILICON APPENDAGE, DO YOU FINALLY UNDERSTAND HIM.
YOU USE HIS RHYTHMIC TRICKS ON JENNY WHILE SHE DIGS HER FINGERS INTO YOUR ASS, LIFTING, SEPARATING, HOLDING YOU HIGH + VULNERABLE. YOU KNOW THAT SHE READ IT IN A FILE THAT...

THEY KEEP ON A TON. PRO-
BABLY FROM SOME BEGGING
SEXT YOU'D SENT; SOME
DIGITAL RECORD OF YOUR
COMPULSIONS, COLLECTED +
RECORDED. YOU DON'T CARE.
PEOPLE ARE WHO THEY ARE +
YOU KNEW WHAT YOU WERE
GETTING INTO. YOU WERE ELEVEN
WHEN YOU FOUND OUT JAMES
BOND WAS BORING. JENNY IS A
BOOKWORM, A NOSEY NANCY DREW.
HER LOVE LANGUAGE IS INTRIGUE.
HER CURRENCY IS INFORMATION.
NANCY WA
BLED BY THE THREAT.
SHE CAN LEARN ANYTHING ABOUT
YOU, EVERYTHING, + SHE SHOWS NO
MORAL RESTRAINT, BUT SHE WANTS
YOU ANYWAY. **AND BRAND NEW.** NOT
BECAUSE YOU'VE ALWAYS BEEN
THERE.
ALL SIGNS OF APOCALYPSE ARE
NIGH - THE FOUR HORSEMEN ARE
HIGH ON THEIR STEEDS. YOU DIDN'T
NEED THE ZOMBIES TO TELL YA.
METEOROLOGISTS HAVE BEEN
WATCHING THE WORLD END IN
SLO-MO, DRIP BY DRIP. WHEN
THINGS GOT FULL ON CRAZY, YOU
COULDN'T HELP BUT TO BE HAPPY
5
FOR MOTHER EARTH, FINALLY SHA-
KING US OFF, LIKE DROPLETS ON
A WET DOG. LIKE FLEAS. THIS
LAST ROUND OF ANTHROPOCENE
WEATHER ENDED WITH AN ATMOS-
PHERIC RIVER, A "RIVER IN THE
SKY". THE NARROW BAND OF HU-
MIDITY STRETCHED FROM
KALAMAZOO TO TOLEDO. FIRST,
IT WAS SNOW; THEN, HAIL. NOW
THE RAIN WAS STRANGELY WARM.
THE GODS ARE PISSING ON US.
YOU MADE THE SLEEP DE-
PRIVED JOKE, **ON AIR**, ...
LIVE

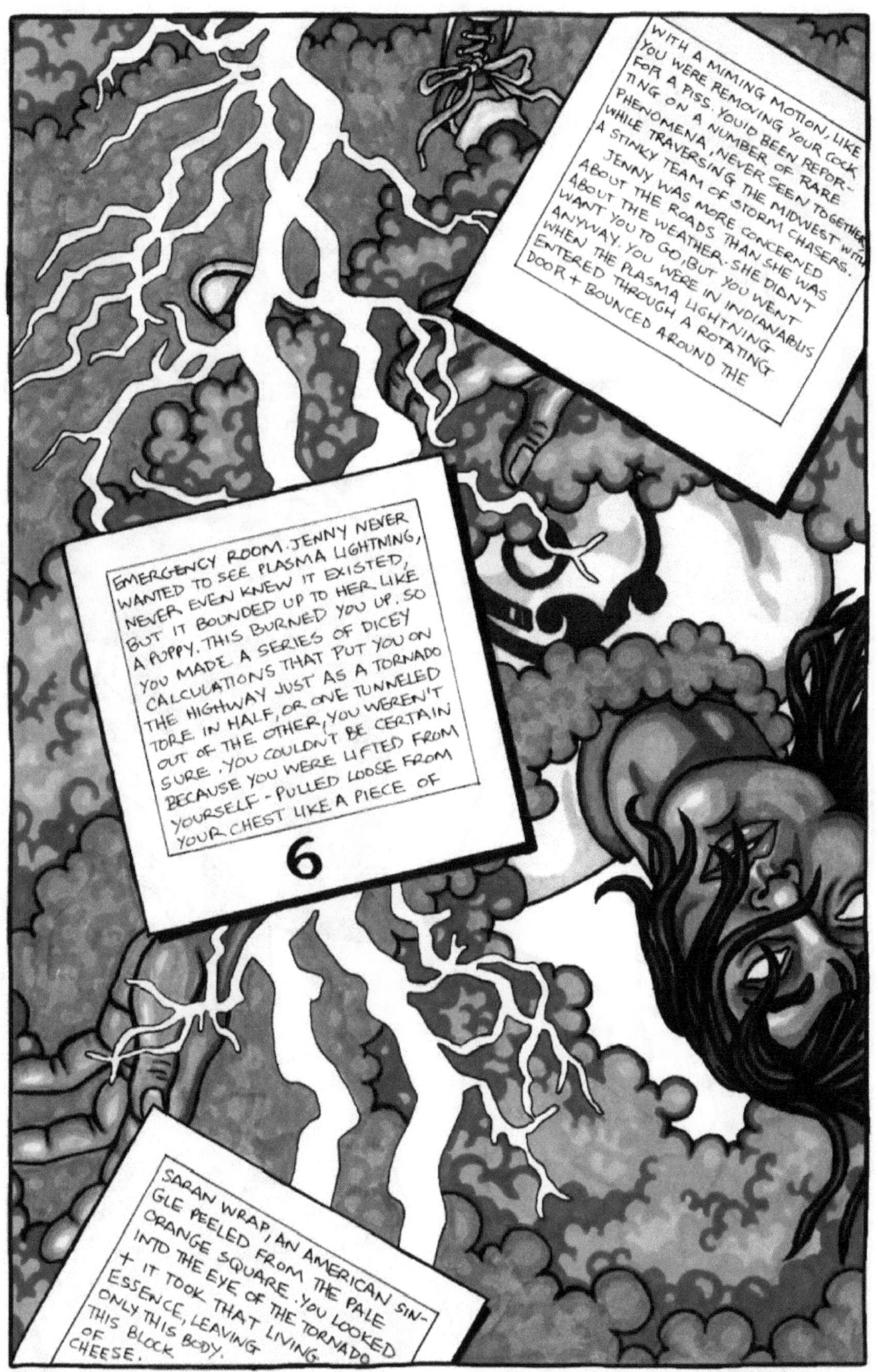
WITH A MIMING MOTION, LIKE YOU WERE REMOVING YOUR COCK FOR A PISS. YOU'D BEEN REPORTING ON A NUMBER OF RARE PHENOMENA, NEVER SEEN TOGETHER, WHILE TRAVERSING THE MIDWEST WITH A STINKY TEAM OF STORM CHASERS. JENNY WAS MORE CONCERNED ABOUT THE ROADS THAN SHE WAS ABOUT THE WEATHER. SHE DIDN'T WANT YOU TO GO, BUT YOU WENT ANYWAY. YOU WERE IN INDIANAPOLIS WHEN THE PLASMA LIGHTNING ENTERED THROUGH A ROTATING DOOR + BOUNCED AROUND THE
EMERGENCY ROOM. JENNY NEVER WANTED TO SEE PLASMA LIGHTNING, NEVER EVEN KNEW IT EXISTED, BUT IT BOUNDED UP TO HER LIKE A PUPPY. THIS BURNED YOU UP. SO YOU MADE A SERIES OF DICEY CALCULATIONS THAT PUT YOU ON THE HIGHWAY JUST AS A TORNADO TORE IN HALF, OR ONE TUNNELED OUT OF THE OTHER, YOU WEREN'T SURE. YOU COULDN'T BE CERTAIN BECAUSE YOU WERE LIFTED FROM YOURSELF - PULLED LOOSE FROM YOUR CHEST LIKE A PIECE OF
6
SARAN WRAP, AN AMERICAN SINGLE PEELED FROM THE PALE ORANGE SQUARE. YOU LOOKED INTO THE EYE OF THE TORNADO + IT TOOK THAT LIVING ESSENCE, LEAVING ONLY THIS BODY. THIS BLOCK OF CHEESE.

GENDER IS IRRELEVANT. WE'RE ONLY A SERIES OF REINCARNATED SOULS, CHURNED OUT LIKE PLAYDOH, SQUEEZING THROUGH THE HOLE IN A STAR SHAPE. OUR PARTS ARE RANDOMLY ASSIGNED. GHOSTS EXIST BEYOND THE BINARY. EXCEPT FOR THE ONES THAT ARE STUCK IN TIME: THE WHITE HAND OF WHITE HAND, OHIO. THEY STOLE HER FROM SLEEP + DRAGGED HER THROUGH THE SNOW, THAT COTTON NIGHTGOWN PULLING UP AROUND HER RIB CAGE LIKE A RUMPLED
FORESKIN, HER PALE BACK WAS BURNED BY FROST, HER HAIR WAS IN ICY TWISTS, YET SHE REFUSED TO SHIVER. YOU BORE WITNESS, THROUGH IT HAPPENED BEFORE YOU WERE BORN. TIME HAS OPENED UP TO YOU IN ITS INFINITE FLUIDITY. GOING TO THE PAST IS ONLY AS HARD AS DIVING AGAINST THE CURRENT, + YOU'VE ALWAYS BEEN A STRONG SWIMMER.
ALL YOUR LIFE, YOU NEVER WANTED TO SEE A GHOST, YOU
7
WERE CLEAR ON THAT. YOU KNEW THAT YOU'D BE UNDONE BY THE EXPERIENCE OF SEEING SOMETHING SO DEVASTATINGLY FAMILIAR. YOU'VE BEEN WALKING FOR SO LONG, YOU SHOULD BE TIRED. YOU SHOULD BE HURTING. THE STORM CHASERS WERE GUNNING TOWARDS I-75 WHEN YOU JUMPED OUT OF A SPEEDING VAN. YOU SHOULD BE BROKEN. ARE YOU?

YOU CIRCLE BEHIND THE OAK, A SHORT-CUT TO THE GRAVEYARD, WHICH IS A MESS OF MELTING ICE + SODDEN GROUND. EACH TOMBSTONE IS A LOOSE TOOTH. YOU BYPASS THE PATH TO YOUR PLACE + HEAD STRAIGHT FOR THE HOUSE ON JUBILEE LANE. YOU MOUNT THE MIRRORED STEPS. YOU'RE POUNDING ON HIS DOOR, WHEN HE ANSWERS, STILL DRESSED. THE WHITE COLLAR IS UNDONE, PLACKET OPEN, NAIL MARKS AT HIS THROAT. "TOUGH DAY, HUH?" HE SQUINTS IN RESPONSE. HE SAYS YOUR NAME LIKE A QUESTION.
"KENDY?"
"SHE'S HERE TO SEE THE DOCTOR." YOU EXTEND YOUR ARM; WRIST, UPTURNED. HE SHUTS THE DOOR ON YOU, NO SURPRISE, BUT RETURNS WITH A STETHOSCOPE. HE SLIPS FROM THE HOUSE TO SHUSH YOU. YOUR HEART BEATS IN HIS EARS, JUST THE CRACKLING SOUND OF A PLASTIC WRAPPER FROM A SLICE OF AMERICAN CHEESE. HE SAYS, "YOU SHOULDN'T BE HERE, KENDRA." YOU CAN'T BE HERE. BUT HERE YOU ARE. HERE HE IS, WITH EVERYTHING JUST
8
SO, EVERY FALLING HAIR, THAT LIFTED EYEBROW, PLUS THE SMELL, EVEN THE HOSPITAL, BUT IT'S NOT ATON. YOU KNOW THIS WHEN ATOM'S EYES WIDEN IN ALARM. ONLY ONE OF THE TWINS SEES SUBTLE ENERGIES, THOUGH YOU'RE NOT SO SUBTLE. YOUR AURA FUNNELS + TUNNELS, BUILDING ENERGY WITH EACH ROTATION. IN YOUR RAVENOUS POWER, YOU'RE KALI. YOU DANCE ON THE SKULLS OF MEN. YOU DEVOUR CORN FIELDS, COWS + MAILBOXES. YOU INHALE A TOW TRUCK; ITS HOOKED TAIL SNAPS IN THE WIND, LIKE A LOOSE ELECTRICAL CABLE.

medusa. – Paris Woodward-Ganz (he/him)

medusa had the right idea i believe.

a cave on a mountain seems the best way to go, watch their eyes as you turn them to stone, hold their lives in the palm of your hand, let no more men tell you what you believe, shatter them and their preconceived notions.

if i was her, i would never leave, escape to where i would be exempt from the rule, the exception
because when a man came into my space and said
i thought you liked this,
all i could say back was,
i was 15,
oh how i wished i had snakes for hair and weapons for eyes,

instead my hair is curly, perfect for someone to grab in their hand and say *you're mine now*, it hurts, that the way of the system that wasn't made for us to succeed will make us bleed to survive, was i made to be broken?

i carry pepper spray with me and plan to go into politics.

sparta would have welcomed us with open arms, a warrior society,
where violence was encouraged and reciprocation too, castrate him with a knife if he touches you,
forget chopping the hydra's heads off, we already know two more grow back in each one's place.

become a vigilante and turn them all to stone, scream at them, and stop playing nice, once
they'd have diagnosed you with hysteria, now they deem you a SJW and pray for your
death.

only through empowerment can anything be changed, with the collective rage of thousands set the world on fire, and dance in the ashes of what remains.

i wish i was medusa, as tragic as her life was, because she at least had an advantage

an advantage that ultimately killed her in the end, because her snakes for hair and weapons for eyes were something that men didn't understand so claiming to be heroes, brought on her demise

Gravediggers Lament – Paris Woodward-Ganz (he/him)

When the stars come out, I think about a lot of things.
Who I am, who I was. Who I want to be.

I am alive to remember, it would be a disgrace to forget. I cannot forget.
In the mirror I see myself but also ghosts, I raise toasts at empty banquet halls illuminated by lanterns, each one representing a soul
that has been lost to time

It's said to heal all wounds, but I carry the scars with me.
What I have lost has mapped itself onto my skin,
I hear news day by day and no longer does it come as a surprise,

this right has been taken away, another trans sibling has died.

Peace is rare these days, it's like we all wait for the other shoe to drop, but we cannot,
will not, go back to how things were in the past.
We will not let others' deaths be in vain,
they carried the burden, we'll shoulder the pain,

and we'll survive with the weight of the world resting upon our backs,
but together we can make all the difference.
I am not the first, I will not be the last

We're drawn to sorrow, like a moth to a flame.

I light a candle. I dig a grave. I dig a grave.

Phobics in the World – Revika Sangamita (she/they)

Hysterical lies and clastic devours
Sensed the cries of the whimsical that snows
And was burned by the latent, by the phobes!

Crimes that spread in eras like filaria
Crimes that spoke louder than the lost utopia
Crimes that bled the ancient pebbles of historia!

That day I was there with "QUEER" on my heart
I was with me finally after all the fallen apart
Still I was called a disgrace instead of an art!

Let the voice filibuster these foreign knowns
Show them the pride and the love we own
Oh let's live our lives and see them turn into stones!

*A version of this piece was previously published by *Live Wire India*

Changing Pronouns: A Step – Revika Sangamita (she/they)

So I changed my pronouns
Exactly what people will pronounce
Instead of the name
RE-VI-KA
Instead of just she, that girl
Or her, her heart
I've added a neutrality
in the flowing feminine river
which by the way I never knew
how it started.
I asked my Instagram followers
to use they/them for me
Along with she/her
So the outcome is she/they
I'll always be that girl
And I'll always be their heart
No matter how much these words change
Someday I might be a he/him, fae/it
I might change my name and
be that person Kerry
Maybe I'll be a lot more than
what I've discovered now
But I'll always be the love that I carry.

Ace – Revika Sangamita (she/they)

No touch can falter this beating heart,
No, you cannot even touch me anywhere
No, this is a sacred palace, and I condemn wholly
About fixing because none of it needs fixation.

Yes, I am not the only one here
Yes, I have nothing against those who do
Yes, I am 18 and I know it
I know I don't feel it, I don't want it
And I still respect the boundaries of S E X.

Maybe, you would have been a little sensitive
A little understandable, A little more generous
But that's maybe only, maybe.

Perhaps the world would be a better place
If you only knew what acceptance is
It's okay if you don't understand,
But that doesn't mean you cannot respect.

I swear, I exist in peace
I live in a dainty harmony with myself
Hope you could see my warmth in the cold world
That I am a spectrum identity of ACE
That I am full of grace
And the sunder you think I am, is nothing but vain.

I am the wonder that I embrace.
Oh dear, I am the wonder that I embrace.

Imagine Girls At Parties – Sara Wiser (she/her/hers)

Imagine girls drinking,
blowing,
sucking,
dancing on elevated surfaces,
tabletops scuffed
and sticky
with footprints
and the silhouettes of youth
and not-so-innocent figurines
and ill intentions.

Imagine me and Ellie and Raquel
at an eight-million dollar
Park Avenue apartment,
mixing whatever we can find,
getting crossed out of our minds,
saying no to blow but still watching the glow of
super rich kids snorting it up their nose.

A girl's jacket catches fire
and we all raise our cups,
screaming at the top of our lungs,
knowing that the cops won't care,
gold tennis bracelets in the air.

She runs into the shower
turning on the water as the clock tower
strikes 4 am
and boys grab boys
and girls grab girls
and someone grabs me by my curls and
kisses me
and kisses Raquel
and kisses Ellie
and suddenly we're all kissing
and suddenly we're all drowning.

It’s your daughters,
sisters,
friends,
ex-lovers
all prostrating themselves
for the attention of anyone
who they know will touch them
in the places they don’t want touched, fooling
themselves into thinking that this is fun.

That this could be love.

Kriah: The Mourning – Sara Wiser (she/her/hers)

CW: References to Grief & Suicide

i.
It's as simple as a tear in my sleeve.

A moment of silence
for her,
for that little girl
who never feared
anything,
not even
herself.

A moment of silence
for the person I once was,
for the girl
who never strayed away
from her own God,
and who never hated herself
so much
that she tried to end it all
on a cold winter day.

ii.
It's as simple as a moment of grief.

I sometimes feel
                    and feel
                              and feel
and I'm afraid
that I'm feeling too much
all at once.

iii.
Sometimes
I think that I might be a phantom,
the ghost of her,
of the girl
who
spun melodies like silk,
who
danced
around her pink-carpeted room at
midnight.

iv.
It's as simple as this:

I spend my waking hours
mourning the person I could have been
If I had never grown up.

I spend my mornings
mourning
a version of myself
that no longer exists.

v.
I sit in silence
and let my coffee go cold
and stare at the wall
and feel
and feel
and feel
it all.

Untitled – Rachel Coyne (she/her)

Untitled – Rachel Coyne (she/her)

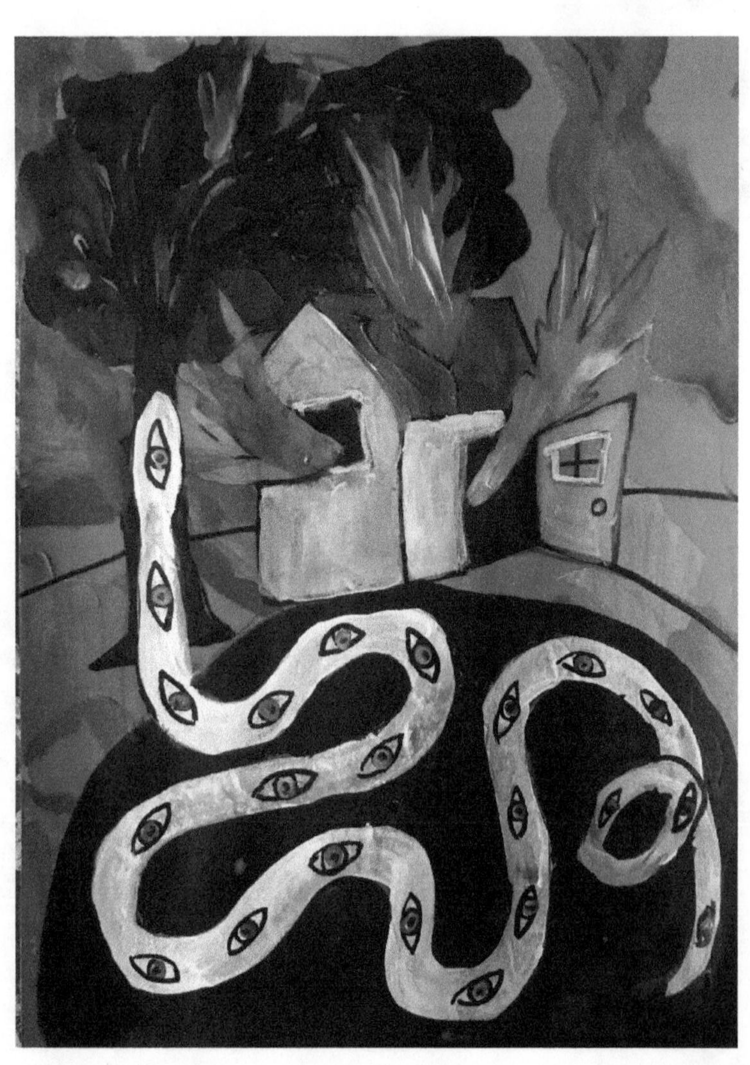

invader – Antonia Rachel Ward (she/her)

tell me your dreams, child
those creations that seduce you—
feverish, deep-core imaginings,
in the thickness of night

tell them to me—
let me examine their soft
petal edges, fragile colour
staining eager fingers

let me dart my probing tongue
into their damp, dark centres
sweet nectar of submerged
desires wet on my lips

let me wrap myself in their folds
cocoon-like, entangling my fibres
with yours until you no longer know
how to unravel us

i am a part of you now
the soul of your organism
coated in your juices and you
will not forget me

mannequin or; the girl with the enamel eyes – Antonia Rachel Ward (she/her)

she was a work of art
a masterpiece, when they decked her out
in white lace and flowers
hair plaited 'round her head.

long lashes,
rose-pink lips.
you look so happy,
they told her.
how could they know he'd painted
the happiness onto her face
layer by layer?

he kissed her tenderly and took her
home.
sat her in the window
for his neighbours to admire.

when she tried to move, he bound
her wrists with golden bracelets.

when she spoke, he sewed
her lips together.

and when her hair fell out, he replaced it
with false tresses, full of lustre.

how does she stay so beautiful?
the neighbours wondered.

while insects crawled
through her gown.

while maggots ate
at her flesh.

and while she sat
at the window
staring unseeing
through enamel eyes.

this is a happy house – Antonia Rachel Ward (she/her)

this is a happy house.
we bought it in summer,
chosen for its quaint, thatched roof
and the flowers in the window box.

it sits in a happy village.
everyone knows their neighbours.
we go to the pub quiz on friday nights,
and church on sundays.

i am a happy wife.
i paint a smile on my face
so no one sees the cracks
in my façade.

this is a happy house.
except for the mould crawling up the walls
and the darkness settling deep
into every corner and crevice.

this is a happy house.
i bury my bones in the garden
and the flowers in the window box
are slowly dying.

starlight – Antonia Rachel Ward (she/her)

starlight, you called her
a heavenly haze—
insubstantial as gas and dust

into my earthly body of decaying cells,
you tried to breathe her galactic glow,
and stood back, admiring how
she burned, white hot,
singeing me at the edges

i could not hold her—
her stellar energy expanded,
consuming my all-too-corporeal mass

i was only human, after all
afflicted by the inevitable
disintegration
of entropy

beneath a celestial weight,
your fantasy collapsed into me

just me, a woman
who will one day fade
to dust

Girl on a Sidewalk//Boys in a Car – Michele Zimmerman (she/her)

One girl walks alone on the frozen sidewalk. She is headed home to her pet wolfhound. She is hungry and she is chilled. She is a girl, so she should know, anything could be coming for her in the murky evening.

***

Four boys drive around in a car at dusk smoking joints and eating drive-through hamburgers. Two of the boys are brothers; the elder has allowed the younger to accompany him and his friends. This is an initiation.

***

Three of the boys saw what to do in a video on the internet. It is a drive-by. It is a flat wooden board like that of their mother's charcuterie plate thrust outside the car window. It is a quick smack to the jaw before the girl can even blink.

The younger brother is unsure that he wants to be a part of this car ride now that he knows what the older boys have planned, but he is cowardly. He says nothing. He breathes in the milky smoke, rolls the rind of a pickle around his mouth. The other boys whistle out the windows, turn on the cameras of their phones. The charcuterie plate is smooth in the younger brother's hands and smells faintly of cheese. The car slows to that of the girl's walking pace.

***

The girl is wrapped in a thick, green coat. Her long hair, wild in the wind, occasionally whips against her face. A leather satchel with schoolbooks and novels and pens is slung across her back. She turns her head, against her better judgement, to look.

***

At the moment of impact, the younger brother realizes he knows the girl from school; she sits beside him in history lecture. She is bigger than a lot of girls in his class. He noticed her because of this. She is rounder and softer, and he likes this, though he would never admit it out loud. He wonders if her softness is the reason his brother has chosen her, or if she is just unlucky enough to be in his older brother's path. He wonders if it matters. Her name is Pearl. He remembers her name.

***

The car speeds away; Pearl holds a hand to her stinging face. She laughs from the shock, her eyes well up with tears. She hopes, desperately, that nobody else is around to have witnessed this event. That this surprise, this embarrassment, can remain secret.

***

The car speeds away; the younger brother vomits into his lap and does not pass the test. His failure before his brother will live with him for the rest of their lives. He is tossed from the car and left to walk home in the dark. An irreparable crack blooms between them.

***

When Pearl makes it home, the wolfhound is waiting for her at the door. Her father works deep into the night. Her brother has abandoned the family to live at his girlfriend's house. Her mother is missing or abducted or runaway or dead and has been for several years. Nobody knows and everyone has stopped wondering, even Pearl.

She and the wolfhound fend for themselves.

She reaches to scratch his muzzle. He licks her hand; he whimpers at her tears. She fills his bowl with food. After he is full, he lets himself out through the hatch in the door. A few moments later, he faithfully returns.

That night she falls asleep holding ice to her cheek, the wolfhound curled under her arm. She wonders what it was that the boys saw when they looked out of their car windows. What exactly about herself made this violence seem welcome?

***

When the younger brother wakes the next morning, he feels his body burning. His throat scratches from vomiting, his feet tingle from walking miles in the cold, and his face stings. He rises from his bed to stand in front of a great full-length mirror framed in mahogany. He opens his mouth to exclaim at the sight of his face, but quickly learns that moving his jaw makes the pain worse.

***

In the morning when Pearl wakes, she turns the camera of her phone onto her own face. She dreads the thought of school, of all the eyes on her as she walks down the hall.

But when she looks in the reflection on the screen, her dread dissolves like sugar on the tongue. She sees where her skin should be splotched the colors of new bruises, it is creamy, unblemished.

***

He stands before the bedroom mirror and examines an eye swollen nearly shut. A jawline darkened purple. A long cut on the cheek, still wet with blood.

"It wasn't my fault," he exclaims to his reflection. "They made me do it, I didn't want to. I promise."

He cries. He cannot recall ever having seen such injuries appear on his brother's skin. He wonders what exactly about himself welcomed such consequences.

***

She touches her skin. The wolfhound yelps with glee, dances circles around her legs. She runs her fingers down her jaw and she is free of all pain. She touches the round circle on the screen and captures the magic of her unmarked face.

***

The school grounds are covered with hoarfrost. Icicles from a late autumn storm dangle from naked tree limbs and stone archways; beadlettes of snow turn the evergreens into ivory pillars. Pearl pulls her coat tighter around her body. She wishes there was someone around, other than her sweet pet, with whom she could share her good fortune.

***

At the entrance of the building, the younger brother pulls a cap down to cover his face. He waits until nearly everyone has gone inside before he steps through the heavy double doors.

On his way to history lecture, he sees Pearl walking down the hall opposite him. He sees the way she walks confidently, her face bare before everyone, and he stops in his tracks.

She wears the same coat as the evening before; her hair is as wild as ever. The curves of her body, visible even through the coat's silhouette, are even softer and more welcoming than he had realized. He knows if he were a different person, if the circumstances were different, he would ask her out.

"These were supposed to be yours," he says instead, and waves a hand over the injuries. "My brother wanted them to be yours."

Pearl stops mid-stride. She recognizes the younger brother's face; she knows she has seen it somewhere. Though she cannot recall where and she cannot recall his name.

She steps close to him and removes the cap. Each can feel the other's breath.

***

With her index finger Pearl traces the younger brother's swollen eye. He flinches at her touch. With a knuckle she presses on his bruised jaw to watch how the colors change. He whimpers. With a fingernail she scrapes the congealing blood of his cut. He watches, his injured eye pushed as wide as it can open.

Pearl takes her phone from the pocket of the green coat. She holds the camera up to his face, and clicks. She shares the image with the waves of the internet.

"So everyone can see," she says, "and wonder what it is about you that makes you so weak."

A Right – Heather Meatherall (she/her)

I have a right to be here
To walk the streets at night
To pick whichever path I like
Not just the one you say is right

I have a right to be here
To love the way I was meant to
And not have to hide just because you
Seem to think it's taboo

I have a right to be here
To feel safe in this body
That despite what you seem to believe
Has only ever belonged to me

I have a right to be here
You may have spent a lifetime
Telling me otherwise
But that does not mean you're right

On Being a Woman in STEM – Heather Meatherall (she/her)

For as long as I've been in this field
And as long as I continue to be
My gender
Will always come before me
Announcing my presence
Defining my difference
My minority is always made
The biggest part of me

I'm a girl who codes
A female computer science student
A woman in stem

And don't get me wrong
I love it
There is community in labels
And I've clung to them
For as long as I've been able to

But there are times
When I wonder what it'd be like
To just be me

A person who codes
A computer science student
Just someone in stem

Funeral Party - Claire Thom (she/her)

The widow,
leading a thread of crisp, clean suits,
watches as the flames eat the pinewood.

He is finally gone.

Ashes to ashes,
dust to dust—
she puts him neatly on the shelf.
Now who's stuck in a box?

She yanks up the shutters
of eyelids, forced shut for far too long,
and grabs this fresh light.

She dusts off her brain cells,
locked in a cell for far too long,
and sweeps away cobwebs
that had entangled her ambitions.

She winks at the clock's face
and grabs time's outstretched hand.

Time on her hands, finally.
Her life before has been tidied away,
along with the albums of mundane memories
and boxes of chores and routine.

She polishes the boredom from the mirror
and reveals a sparkling reflection.
She reflects on this image
of an old stranger before her.
Before him
and his story—
what was her story?

She irons out the crisp, clean paper.
Now there are no more crisp, clean shirts to iron,
only this bold, blank page.

Inky waters begin to race down transparent
flumes
and words shoot out in splashes
of liberated creative power
and joyful triumph.

Something Up My Sleeve – Claire Thom (she/her)

The bell rattles—
we´re released for break.
I make my way out the door,
weave through a throng of students,
crimson nails curled round the cuff
where it´s carefully stuffed.
Hoping I make it in time,
I climb the stairs, heels clicking.
I quicken my pace, pale face and
pounding pain deep in my belly.
I finally reach the safe sanctuary
of the toilet—
fling open the door,
pray there´s paper.
The clack of the latch—
I let out a massive exhale
and red drops
of relief.

Grasp - Sarah Ray (she/her)
—After Vievee Francis

"No one wants to have a breast biopsy.
But it's good to remember that 80%
of women who do have a breast biopsy
do not have breast cancer." —A patient's Guide to Breast Biopsy

With practiced fingers
those careful hands
ushered me into a robe
ultrasound slime and wand
pressed into my chest

I tried to swim away
in my mind
to look at something else—
the speckled ceiling tiles,
but caught on a line,
I saw the crescent-shaped,
framed-black
circle of unknown mass.
I asked:

What is that?

She told me not to worry
and kept moving the wand,
eyeing around inside my breast,
flattened and stretched from
nursing babies

I felt cold

my body gifted me
with a second
mass of cells
that shouldn't exist
I existed there again

drowning
on that table, looking inside
the black and white of me,
the part of me that sustained
two lives from the milk of me,
now sustaining another
dark part of me,
there to consume the
trance of life inside of me,
sinking into a wide lake,

is there a part of me
I get to keep?

Before the inevitable I attempt to
hold myself in

and I wait.

I remember there is only a
twenty percent
chance
of this sinking
its hook in me and
catching the air
in my lungs.

I spent a week believing – Sarah Ray (she/her)

I had cancer
in my breast,
a second time.
The first time,
it was deep
inside my chest.
Nestled
behind bones,
caged
into my heartsong.
I waited for the phone
to ring. This body
of stone,
full of disease—
a death threat
whispered
from behind
for seven days,
I could think
of nothing else
until I was told
that whispered
threat
was benign.

I Know Nothing About Being Alive – Sarah Ray (she/her)

"I really can't explain it, being alive and all." —*Mary Ruefle*

She loves me pieced together,
whole, but she doesn't know that.
My daughter watches me
drop colorful pills into the yellow
pill organizer while she sings
the days of the week.
A calendar of my aliveness encapsulated
in yellow plastic time.
She reassures me, I have one piece
of the puzzle in each day.
She hovers.
I say, *I love you.*
Instead of, *this is too hard.*
Instead of,
I don't want to talk about this anymore.
Because, I don't really know anything about
living.

In my parents' house there was no talk
of yellow calendars full of missing pieces.
There was always
I love you
(I don't want to talk about this anymore.)
I didn't know how to ask about living so,
I stuck my toes
through my mother's afghan and hoped
instead of living, my dying might be noticed.
Dying there alive, not knowing
what to say when
there was nothing to talk about anymore.

My toes dug into my mother's thighs through
the holes in acrylic string like roots searching for water.

They called it daydreaming,
my head in heaven and my toes in the earth.
        I had to keep digging to find
a calendar full of Sunday, Monday,
        Tuesday, Wednesdays—
every day that could be sung, squatting over
            the pieces built from planting myself
so that I could know what it was like to be alive.

Misfired Synapses – Sarah Ray (she/her)

When I was seven, I stained the carpet outside my first-grade classroom with the contents of my stomach. I had experienced the first headache where I could feel my heartbeat inside my eye. There would be more that would send me to hospitals. More that would send me through imaging tubes that show the black and white images of the place where fear is kept. First, my mother searched for answers. Then, I was on my own without answers, spiraling into medications that didn't work. Those years were veiled in a curtain pulled at the edges by pain, spent in darkness. I saw only the light my brain created for itself in misfired synapses. I heard a song repeating, scratched at the key change. I would eventually find a solution. I had to accept it would also chip away at my mind. It made mosaics out of the words I loved—my memory, the poetry of me. In its confusing beauty it kept the pain away. Daily, it kept me from numbness and stumbling along the sharp edges of dying. So I welcomed the round, pale yellow chances at life, placing them into their daily time slots to keep me out of hospitals, out of trouble, and misery. I welcomed the chance to rest and realize that I am whole now, held together by a child's amount of school glue and masking tape.

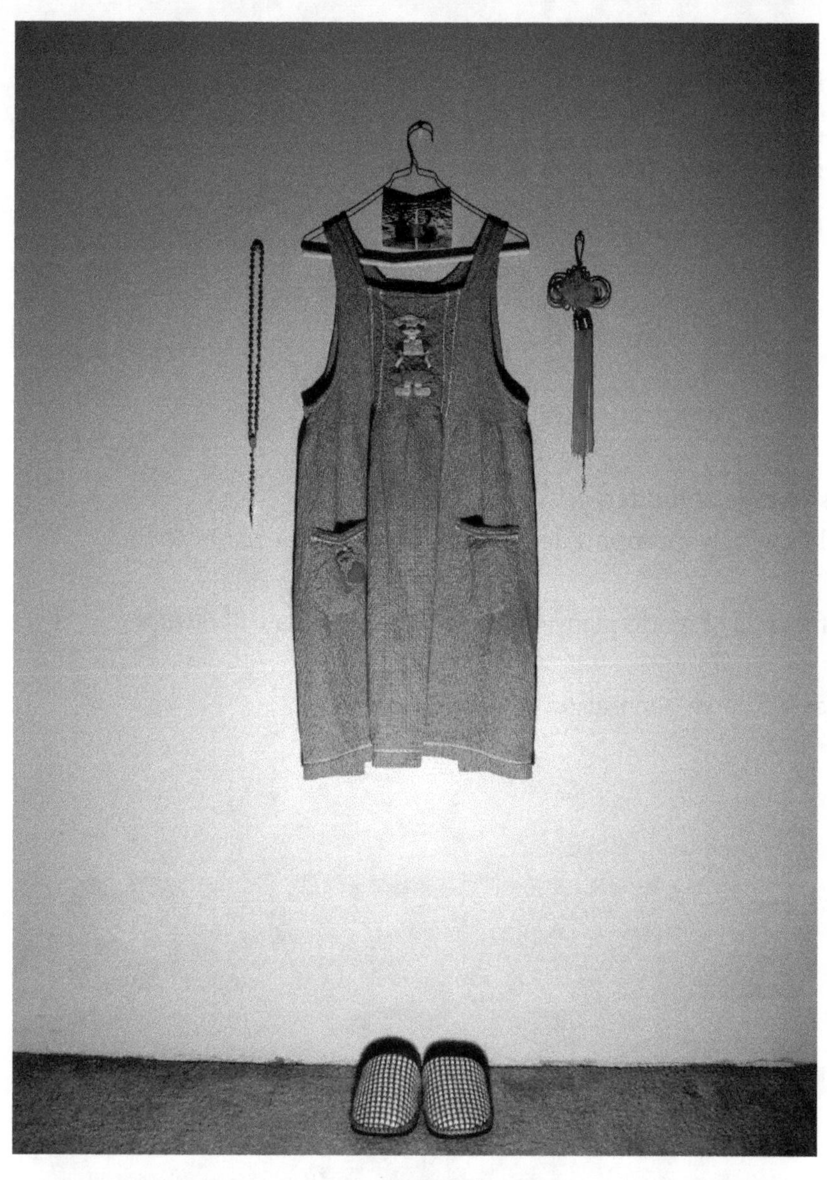

A Moment of Omens – Julie Lee (she/her)

Her Mother's Daughter – Veronica Szymankiewicz (she/her)

She is her mother's daughter,
engaged in eternal self-warfare.
Total annihilation...
A grueling ritual,
culminating in absolute spirit slaughter.
Blood is definitely thicker than water.
It runs quite deep and there is never any shortage of fodder,
for an unstoppable, soulless marauder unknowingly intent on decimating her lineage exactly as they taught her.
Insidious low self-esteem, incapacitating feelings of inadequacy, and perpetual doubts will always gnaw away at her, making her falter.
A cursed psychological family heirloom passed down generation to generation,
from mother to daughter.

Witches – Veronica Szymankiewicz (she/her)

All lined up in a pretty little row,
all tied up with a pretty little bow.
Tempers rising and accusations flying,
a horror show set up to gleefully watch others dying.
They are the renowned witches of lore,
cast into fires while being called a whore.
They are the women who used their inherent gifts,
to bring about necessary paradigm shifts.
They are the women who used their voices,
believing everyone had a right to their own choices.
These are the women who bore children and labored for their communities,
sharing their blessings and life-changing opportunities.
They are the ones who helped others while giving everything they had,
until one day the tide turned and all the good they did was labeled bad.
They were beyond brilliant and strong,
therefore it meant they were evil, as well as wrong.
Punished for crimes they did not commit,
by those who couldn't admit, they didn't have an ounce of their grit or quick wit.
Condemned to burn for their knowledge of nature and the human condition,
refusing to bow down in submission for
completing their soul's mission.
Tied to a stake on the pyre,
they looked into the eyes of each and
every grotesque liar.
Those who gathered in the crowd,
whose self-hatred was loud, proud, and worn like a shroud.
The women smiled in united rebellion,
might as well go out like a hellion.
Invoking favors from the goddesses,
as the flames rose hungrily up their bodices.
They called on Hecate and Oshun,
they called on Kali Ma and the Moon.
They summoned the elements from their four corners—Earth, Water, Fire, and Air,
asking them to hear their prayer.
The scent of burning flesh wafting through the Salem breeze,
the onlookers infected with humanity's disease,
salivating as if this spectacle was just a striptease.
The witches did not give them the satisfaction of a show,
instead the sisterhood stood together stoically staring at those below.

You see, even in death they would not be silent or compliant,
their blood still runs through the veins of the women today who are defiant and self-reliant.
Throughout history we have been called the witches and the bitches,
by anyone who saw us as too big for our britches.
We have been burned, hanged, and stoned,
we have been beaten, raped, and owned.
Yet, here we still stand,
our power is our brand,
The divine feminine is light, love, sensuality, and darkness,
as well as creation, destruction, and anything but starkness.
Our magic flows as we dance with our shadows,
fuck those who oppose, yelling that we're stepping on their toes.
You can love us, hate us, or fear us for who we are,
but we'll be damned if you think you can just steal the magic contained in our collective grimoire.
We are the witches and the bitches who will not stand down on command,
as we continue to fight, crowns on our heads and sharpened swords in hand.

Holy Animal – Mimi Flood (she/her)

God bites the girl on her inner thigh
So she fish hooks him through his cheek
as she brings him closer
Drops of blood fall on her body.
Are you afraid? She asks.
He mumbles.
Because I'm not even close, she says

Happy Birthday To Me – Mimi Flood (she/her)

While you were
Getting married
On my birthday.
I was
Performing fellatio.
In baby pink lipstick.

Pop Goes the Weasel – Mimi Flood (she/her)

I was happy—
I mean I was pretty much okay
Until he ripped away any chance of me not to suffer from ptsd.
Everything was loud. The walls were pulsating like it was my heart.
I was semi lucid, but when I came to, my mouth was open and my panties were gone.
He asked if I wanted to go somewhere.
I don't know why I said yes but we ended up at a diner.
He sat across from me. He was smiling and talking.
What happened started to process and flash.
I just kept getting angrier by the second.
The shame. The guilt of taking a drink from him. He was my fucking
friend. I feel different now. I'm not the same. I wanted him to feel everything.
All of my fucking rage!
Then his head popped. His blood was all over me.
I let out a laugh and smiled. Drank my milkshake.

The Slide Down the Highway – Mimi Flood (she/her)

All alone in
a cold sweat.

All these lines
on my hand
connected
to nothing

Green, purple veins
in envy

It's so hard to tell
someone to stay
how they stained
my skin
when they leave
it leaks through
my blood
crippling my heart.

Have you ever jumped
out of your skin?
Found yourself
on top of a hill?
The sun barbequing
my jaws, peeling my
skin around the
corners of my
mouth and eyes

I have a hole inside of me
I just want someone's hand to
cover it

When it hides
I have a clear view
of the long slide down
to the highway

16 – Mimi Flood (she/her)

I knew when I was young.
At 16 I tattooed my name in Times New Roman across my collarbone.
Underneath my birthday scratched. I took a razorblade and added Blue ink.
My social security number Implanted in roman numerals in my forearm.
Feet in dirt mud and the water above calm and steady But I knew better.
The sun percolated my skin.
Nude, I took off the bandage of my Last tattoo
My mother's address on my stomach.
Two weeks of healing.
Underneath, I love you in braille.
I walked in, closed my eyes, and held my breath.

My Sisters – Kamilah Mercedes Valentín Díaz (she/ella)

Treated like a bouquet
                    of flowers
treasured for a time
plucked in their prime

rotting from the inside
                    out.
Slated
          to be tossed aside.

Cotización – Kamilah Mercedes Valentín Díaz (she/ella)

Me exigieron,
        -Ponte linda.

¿Ponte?

Expliquenme, ¿Cómo es que alguien se puede poner linda?

No es como poner la mesa
        Tenedor a la izquierda
        Cuchillo a la derecha
        Con el plato entremedio
        Y los vasos arriba del punto del cuchillo
        Señalando como flecha

Mi belleza no es una prenda
que se quita a tu gusto.

Tampoco un interruptor
de luz bajo tu mando.

Prefiero adornarme con ganas
no por obligación.

Todo con puritita intención.

Me cuestionan,
        -¿Te maquillaste?
        -¿Te arreglaste el pelo?
        -¿Te vas a poner eso pa' salir?

Si me pinto la bemba es mi decisión.

La estrella del show
brillo con mi propio flow.

Si no te gusta el color
aparta tu mirada corazón de melocotón.

Te peinas o te haces rolos.

Que yo siempre
valgo oro.

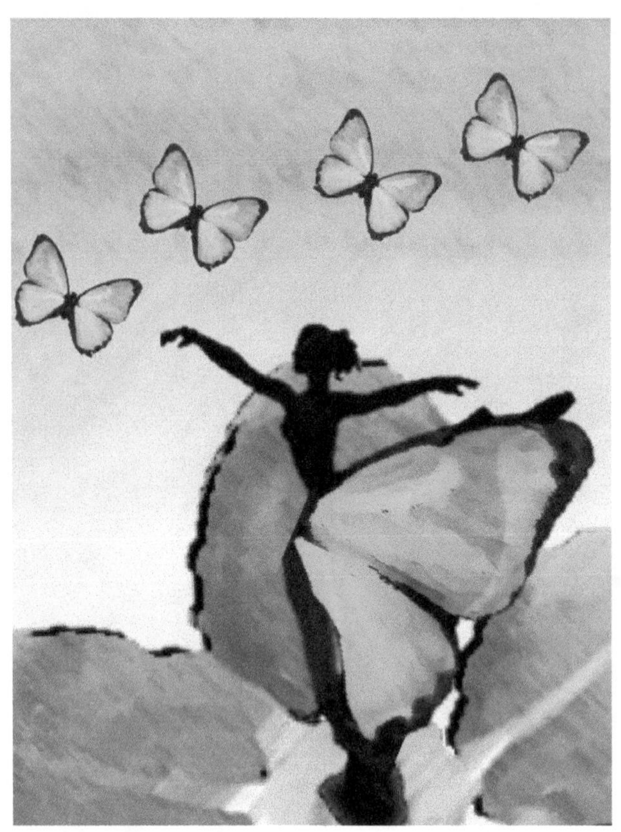

Ballet of the Forget-Me-Nots – S. Kavi (she/her)

Young & Green – S. Kavi (she/her)

Lady Monarch – S. Kavi (she/her)

Blossom – S. Kavi (she/her)

Reunited – S. Kavi (she/her)

Pet the lion – Sarah Merrifield (she/they)

As an adult I had to learn how to stop being afraid of the dark
My tarot keeps telling me to face my shadow self
Pet the lion
I have recurring dreams I am being devoured by wild cats
I look for symbols but fail to follow them
I am looking for the light that is not there
Begging for sleep, another day
Pushing aside the platter of all I choose to not face
Why is it I am having the same nightmares as a child?
Why do I have the same fears?
What struck me so young—
Kept me so young—
Learning to cope however I could fathom
Survival isn't a lifestyle
I am always turning a corner on who I think I am
Who knew adults could be afraid of the dark?
Who knew kids could endure so much and seem so adult?
Who knew adults could endure so much and seem so child?
Maybe all these birthdays I have celebrated have been a parody
The day will never truly dawn on me until I accept dusk
Remember the universe does nothing personal, nature makes no attacks
It is all just a mental drama
And I am detaching myself more everyday from the repeated stories that have kept me from awakening
I am speaking the fears I thought too cursed to pronounce
By way of making them seem both real and valid, and constructed and vapid.

Obituary – Sarah Merrifield (she/they)

I've been divorced from the question of what I want and married to what I think people want me to do for so long I can't even feel rightness in my bones anymore. It feels foreign and I must shut it down, lest an insurgence begin. Lest a revolution begin. It's too dangerous to prioritize my spirit. It involves too many goodbyes. Too much nostalgia swept under the rug. I've evaded the work for so long it has piled up and built walls around my home to where even this isn't safe. You can't run forever. You can't deny the truth forever. It will all start to bleed through your walls, it will show on your flesh and your bones will puncture your skin and your life will be incarnated. You will die anyways. You might as well die doing what you love. You might as well live a little before. I've convinced myself there isn't much time left, but every easy breath I take opens me up to the possibility I was wrong. Honestly, I hope I've been wrong about a lot of things; I hope the universe doesn't want me dead and all of the bad things aren't going to happen to me just because I can't stop thinking of them. I hope the universe sends me every lesson I need whether that's in the shape of a flower or a bruise because I'm starting to remember what matters again. The development of my spirit. The releasing of my wounds. There's something more than what I've claimed to be; no one quite understands but every moment I feel it culminating a little more, a tide rising inside where the words don't reach. Every moment is drawing me closer to my destiny. If I doubt a single second I disrespect all the intricate magic it took to get me here, and that's a poem I'm not prepared to write. That's an obituary.

i killed the cis girl i was – Roya Motazedian (they/them)

is it wrong of me to have pitied you
or rather
to have absolutely fallen
for the way you stood tall
soaking up all the sun
for yourself
and knowing that you were worthy
of every ray?

babe
i'm sorry.
i couldn't help
but start growing right next to you
growing taller
so i could stare into your
precious eyes
my dear
your eyes are flower fields
of their own
bearing different colours and scents
as you stare at me
eyes full of water
as you stare at me
as i watered the flowers
in your eyes
i could only see
how pretty they were
but i couldn't see
your pain

i'm sorry.

i didn't realize
that me growing next to you
would mean i would steal all your
soil
sun
water became
mine
but i thought you were
fine
because of the flowers in your
eyes

i didn't
realize
that you couldn't live off of
only me
like i thought you could

so here i am
a weed
standing tall
having taken your spot
left with nothing but your
remains
that i'm beginning to
consume
without even wanting
to
but simply because
that's how i can
live

i'm sorry.

you were hurting
inside
and i failed to
realize
mistaking your winter
storms
for light april
showers
i lost you to my own
ignorance
i thought you were
fine
because i was
fine
i thought the sunflower would
survive
even if the weed grew next to
her
but we couldn't have the symbiotic
relationship
that i dreamed of having
with you.

Certain Lines – Rachel Mulder (she/her/hers)

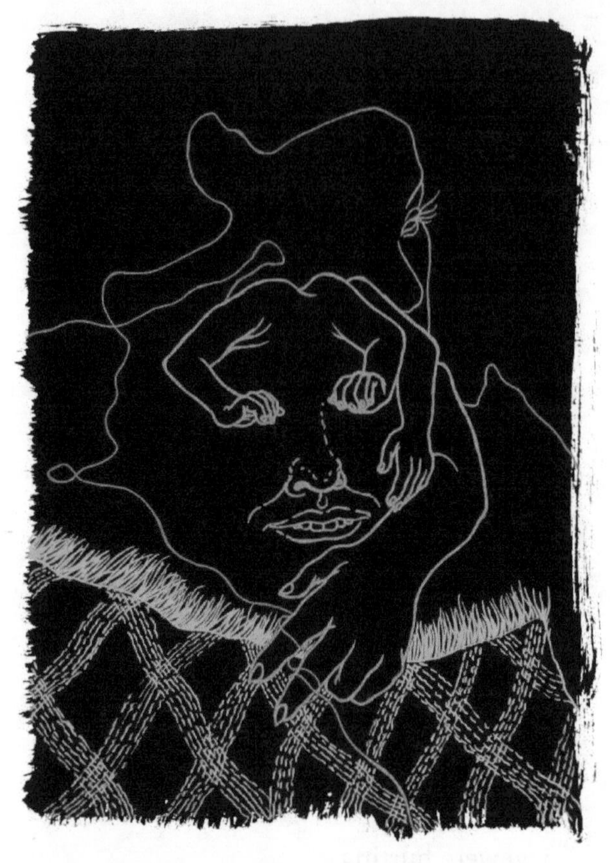

Cowardly Messages – Rachel Mulder (she/her/hers)

Sisterly Glaces – Rachel Mulder (she/her/hers)

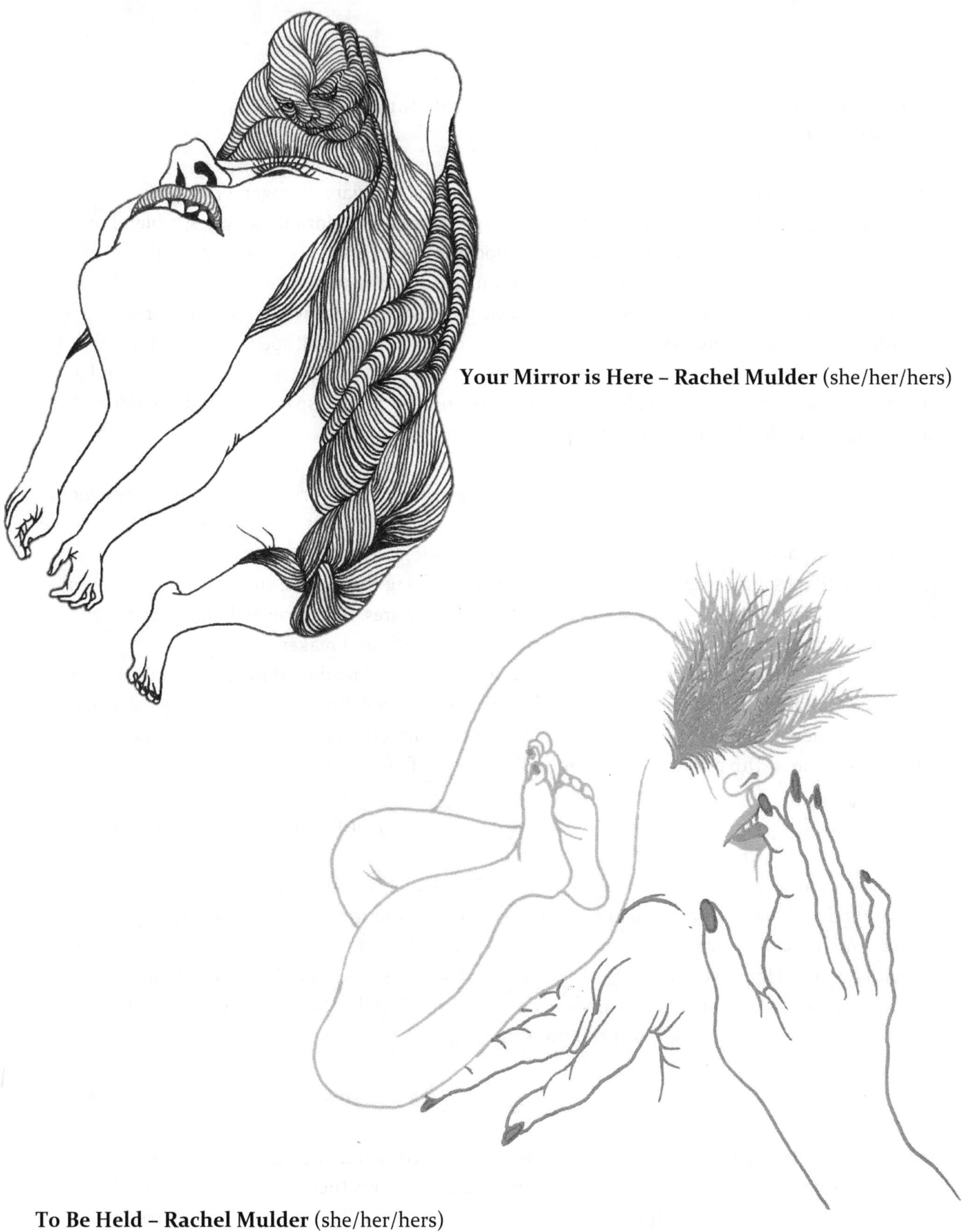

Your Mirror is Here – Rachel Mulder (she/her/hers)

To Be Held – Rachel Mulder (she/her/hers)

a poem about the flight & fight to win the right to vote for women ::
on suffrage, seeds, & stuff – Jen Schneider (she/her)

october :: dusk turns to dawn. calendar pages continue to cycle. aviary arrangements sprout (exponentially) in soil and sky. skies beam rays both gregarious and glorious. all hues, a blend of mocha and happenstance. all months monitored. flocks in flight. broken wings ready to fly. miles to climb. miles and milestones rarely conquered in minutes (or moments). mates and dates tangle in autumn leaves. hues of crimson, chocolate, and kelly green vines dance with clovers of three (sometimes four) leaves. late nesters linger. mourning doves meander. all species industrious, multiple broods banter. autumn winds tango as souls in soles stir. march (1) both a moment and a state of being. advocacy and advocates nest (no time to rest) in nimble spaces. worms wonder and wander. inch by inch. ideas rustle in small pockets of air.

migration a cycle of moments turned minutes turned memories

january :: broods and broads battle winter winds. limbs lock in layers. flannels and feathers spread heat and traction (amidst multiple factions). stray branches sag then settle. snow and snowy doves accumulate inches and inklings. icy stares battle household wares. flocks follow land (destinations ripe with anticipation). migration routes make room for movers and makers. instincts and imaginations trace tracks and new trails. species both sapiens and feathered funnel (and flock) areas and avenues (2) of aspiration and inspiration. spherical lens travel distances both documented and undeclared. binoculars reveal patterns of primed propositions. all prepositions inked. all feather (& fonts) focused. brea(d)th reveals lines (often well defined) of life and limits.

music a migration of curiosities turned chirps turned cycles

march :: baby chicks are born with wings in fetal positions. all feathers combed. flaps and fledglings eager for food and flight. parades and propositions of paramount importance. all nests, targets. Parasites and predators persist. March winds / lion's roars / both a memory and a moment (3) limbs light with bounce. Hops taken in stride. All gaits a gander. All gazes grounded. Longer legs make for faster walking. all steps, a blend of ideas stewed on a slow boil. puffs (breath both bated and weighted) simultaneously stoke travel and transgressions.

flight a symphony of notes turned north stars

april :: nests constructed of twig, twine, and time nurture. brush and bristles protect. persistence wrapped in paper dolls (dna linked across regions) and linen layers (needles and knots resemble patterns inked and linked in compilations). shadows linger. the vigilant seize victories. sized of varying containers (plastics on the horizon / paper puddles and pools). small and large gaits gain traction. all nests, a process. all beaks, a tool. all builds, a beacon. foundations and flocks, often fragments (and fragmented) of wind and wonder.

distance decorated of flight, food, and feathers

july :: planted seeds sprout. sticks tangle. symphonies conduct canopies of crushing beauty. rush hour a july sky. conductors wave wands of fire and ice. lightning chases thunder. asteroids and constellations clash. meters & meteorites gain attention. all senses engaged (some enraged). all birds, blue (time & tin both chased & chasing transformation). young raised (4) in pre-existing nesting cavities. all wings, ready for flight.

danger a dance of daisies, distance, and destination

august :: efforts of june (turned july), and many moons (in perpetual rotation) (5) perform. all the world's a stage. advocacy as much art as aviation. cycles spin with carousels. all ponies freshly painted. all saddles taken. lyrics linger in air heavy of salt and sauerkraut. four-legged mammals, a loyal companion. barks both warning and waning.

anger and danger a difference of a single degree turned letter

gregorian.calendars.cycle.curiosities.spin.carousels.turn.pages.of.time.september.october.november.december,january.february.march.april.may.june.july.august.september.the.gregorian.calendar.both.divided.and.united.of.days.and.destinies.long.and.layered.all.days.to.suffer.both.a.state.of.being.and.a.reason.to.be.more.than.simply.to.be.gregorian.calendars.continue.to.cycle.spin.turn.

1. souls in rubber soles march (make) through / of history (1915)
2. march both a moment and a momentum
3. parade routes neither routine nor regulated (1913)
4. babes in never never land toy with prepositions & propositions
5. moons orbit earth / earth orbits sun / calendars cycle and spin / souls in rubber soles continue to march

To Tell or Not to Tell / At the Intersection of Motherhood and Creativity
Recollection, Documentation, Redefinition – Jen Schneider (she/her)

I. Recollection

/ˌrekəˈlekSH(ə)n/

noun

1. the action or faculty of remembering something.

I have no mementos of childhood. No documents. No photos. No crayoned pictures. No self or family portraits (neither Kodak instant prints nor digital designs). No shoeboxes stuffed of secrets (neither origami notes from faded back-pockets nor postcards clipped to fit in faux-silver lockets). No locked diaries with missing keys. No first poems (neither sonnets nor elegies). No composition book scribbles (of cursive print inclines). Neither color-by-number or connect-the-dot scrambles. Not even the work that I wrote for a contest and won. A coveted gift certificate worth ten dollars at the local Hallmark store. The one in a small strip mall, to the left of the Clover (now defunct). No four-leaf clovers (hand pressed). No quarterly report cards (mostly As, I confess). I spent every penny of my winnings on sheets of stickers that we'd trade at lunch. That were later stolen. By someone I had trusted.

Along with motherhood memories. Homemade. Freshly laundered. Bleached. Under-stuffed. Memory both fallible and fickle. Motherhood the ultimate generator as well as disseminator of recollection. Perspectives layered. Literature suggests, then tells us in glossy eight and a half by eleven print, that we forget. Quickly. Reliably. Curiously. Data only as good as the day it's received. With each passing moment turned minute turned want-to-hold event, memory becomes less reliable. So easy to circumvent. Like the heavily photoshopped images in the popular magazines. Deceiving. Yet the literatures also suggests that these moments can be revealed, and, when prompted, recollections can be reclaimed and redressed.

Hidden deep in the recesses of brain matter and present-day things that matter. If not more, they are certainly more pressing. Ankles peeking from outgrown fleece. Dishes in sinks. Congealed noodles. Concealed quarters. Lottery tickets and homecomings all have a price. Conversations woven of syllables on ice. Finely chopped. Heavily diced. Direction as much recollection as confection. Confectionary sugars. Cinnamons. And spice.

This year I hope to find and reclaim them through writing. To capture life midstream. So that I can later recollect and retrieve. The magic that happens when a single leaf (loose, wide, and college-ruled) floats with an unexpected breeze. Maple or oak. Four-leafed clovers. Children on skates. Babies on wobbly legs. The dash of limbs. The rash of surprise. Spontaneous triggers. Recollection on ice. I'll cool them. Secure them. Freeze them in ink. Preserve the flurries, the gusts, the bouquets of scented thinks. On the grill. Of the daily grind, Routines and rituals sautéed and simmered. Summer lemonade. Sweet and sour. Both divine. Uniquely mine.

I pledge to capture the moments in journals on journeys. To reclaim the tastes. No minutes to waste. The flavors of the children's potato knishes and home-baked matzo ball dishes. The sound of denim-covered legs peddling tricycles with rainbow streamers. Strawberry patches on knees. Ceramic dishes full of steamers. The scent of *Tide*. Lilac in layers of cotton and lace. The flavor of dishes garnished of parsley. Seasoned of cumin. Served over rice. The scent of fresh grass by open windows. Sidewalks of chalk. Pastel and sublime. Silhouettes carefully traced. Angels in snow boots. Turnips with pulled roots. Memory intact. Lists of facts. Spiral notebooks by the dozen. Bakers inclined. Allergies and allergens. Alliterations across time.

II. Documentation

/ˌdäkyəmənˈtāSH(ə)n/

noun

1. material that provides official information or evidence or that serves as a record.

2. the process of classifying and annotating texts, photographs, etc.

I also hope to write to not only recollect, recall, and reclaim but to document. Diaries of days. In original ways. New to me. I'll wait and see. To remember my own children's firsts. Seconds. Thirds. Pasts. I'll layer lists with letters. Heavily spiced. Adjectives and adverbs. All things nice. I'll season all seasons (winter.spring.summer.fall) with details (wide and tall). Both delicate and dangerous. No need to throw caution to the wind. I'll stream lyrics that linger (Dolly and Lynn) while I lose myself in recollections that will transform and transition to carefully composed melodies of documentation. I'll seize the clichés. Curate them on my time. The beauty of memories documented is that they are mine. Universal truths of individual inclinations. Notions of unity. Tokens of tradition.

First blushes. Cheeks on fire.
Ah choo (tissues on re-issue). Cows that moo.
Children atop wagons. Horse-drawn. Red Flyer.
First bonfires. Smoky air.
The feel of the marshmallows melting.
The touch of the flea market chair.
Wicker and wonder. Wisdom teeth removals.
Nervous firsts (school, commutations). Nerve regeneration.

Scooped soil with dowels. Sorted, soiled towels.
Collected drips. Denim rips. Chaffed knees.
Sweat and sweet recollections.
Hide and Go Seek under weeping willow trees.
Wisdom passed down through generations.
The words she used when gifting me her rocker.
The tone of her voice when she'd answer the phone.
The manners of address—*Hi, Doll.*
What's that? Who's there? Words I long to hear.
Conversations on commutes.
Commutations and birthday celebrations.
Yellow cake. Yellowed drapes.
Fresh rolls—warm. Aged cheese—thinly sliced.
The stuff of life. All corners tucked.
Tattletale gray. Collars and Roots.
Accelerated mute buttons (and mutations).
The doctor's scribble.
The tech's whisper.
First time list. Last time list.
The last shared meal.
Jars of Miracle Whip.
Gifted buttons. No matches.
Sifted parkas—plaid and puffers. No clashes.
Door knockers. Tartan knickers.
Souls in rubber soles. No sneakers.
Softball pitches. Hard ale pitchers.
The stuff of life. Some days sweet. Others heavy with strife.
The roadside pit stops.
The inevitable highway delays.
The scent of their new room.
The smell of loss that always comes too soon.
A rainbow of fabrics. Confetti hues. In fresh notebooks and frequented Google drives. From the road. On the train. Sitting at a stop sign at the corner of broad and main. Not simply dates or days. But the layers of scents, sounds, timbres.
Hope for writing as a way to remember. To be present and to gift myself the documents for a future day.

III. Redefinition

/ˌrēˌdefəˈniSH(ə)n/

noun

1. the action or process of defining something again or differently.

I also plan to tell my story. My side. My nuances. My scents and sensibilities. The nuances. The wrinkles. All mine. Perspectives as variable as pancakes. Batter fresh. Knowing there's no chance or time to rewind. Not for a traditional show and tell. But as a tool to track (perhaps taunt) testimony and time.

Amidst relentless tracked changes and redlines. Refine / Redefine. I'll redefine what it means to create. Forego word counts and focus on words.

Track themes of all tenses. Favored and savored. Past. Present. Future. No verbs irregular. No nouns possessive. The ink will unite and mitigate memory oversight.

As the days grow shorter and daylight savings draws near, I begin with a list. One I'll hold close to my chest. Baked of memories all mine. And time. Destiny, I know, can turn on a dime. Phone calls conveying final breaths. Texts with dates for final rests. I've consumed and received, yet never fully processed. Trained to please. Now I collect and curate hopes, from 1 to ten, for a year ahead. At the intersection of motherhood and creativity, I confront challenges on their head and write through tears and tired muscles after everyone else goes to bed.

1. Embrace the rhyme. I've always had a penchant for rhyme. Sprinkled amidst free verse. Planted before (and after) prose. Even flash can stand a dash (both em and __).
2. Personalize the grind. Find a groove. Not all schedules need to be moved. Seize the small pockets of air between Here and There. In note apps and pencil pocket pads. Receipts and napkins. Not all sniffles bad. Stay present. In the moment the gurus and self-help guides suggest. I will. As a tool to observe and document.
3. Puree obstacles (like bananas and chili) into opportunities.
4. Read labels, both regular and rare. Keep a book in all pockets. Always prepare.
5. Maintain a right to reflect and to backtrack. Write in and through detours (also doors). Both closed and open.
6. Find fruit not yet ripe then isolate. Bake in sun drenched sills. Supplement with vitamin d pills
7. Encapsulate I'm capsules. Notes and hand drawn battles. Digital divides persist and exist in five star WiFi's designs.
8. Pregnant pauses cause no pain.
9. Write in the rain. Under tarps in tirades.
10. Consume Vegetables in families market stands off main

11. Don't pull bandages too tight. Not on one's self. Not on one's offspring.
12. Shelf books are as prime as table books.
13. Resist pressure to tell. Writing cathartic and revealing both private and—-

1. A favored...
2. ...

To Recollect, Document, and redefine / amidst relentless tracked changes and redlines. Refine / Redefine

To Document, Declare and ___ Deliver

1. A favored...

Re creativity

an elegy (re)framed & (re)plated as "i'm sorry" / censorship made of both self and salve – Jen Schneider (she/her)

in the Jewish faith—hello, joseph / hello, ruth
hello, Miriam—recollections linger from camps
of (no) tomorrow—the day of atonement
occurs on the 10th day of Tishrei, ten days
after the start of Rosh Hashanah (the Jewish
New Year). Yom Kippur is the holiest day
of the year. observers reflect, repent for sins,
& fast from nightfall to nightfall. mourning
doves chirp blessings from outdoor sills.
observers refrain from work (the faithful)
and consumption (the bait & pull). in personal
recollections (ultimately fickle & flawed) fasts
are traditionally (less typically) initiated with
meatballs sweet and sour / pickles dill and kosher
& broken with smoked fish and vegetables (elders
pick). all freshly skinned. recipes for chopped
liver and gefilte fish remained sealed of bitter
herbs, secret kicks, and salted kisses. most years
i'd sit in silence and consume with little regret (tales
of nursery rhymes turned Judy Blume finds). My
bottom hidden in plaid & denim / sugar cookies
in a snoopy-themed jar. now i don't even try
to read. my mind on overdrive. fully grown,
the nest long flown. thoughts of time
spent in small kitchens / of the east and west,

recipes: ### ingredients
pasts: st(k)icks ###

our days were full of stories as much as apologies
/ plucked and packaged. over-cooked beef. under-
seasoned weekly checks. salted salmon and horse
radish cream cheese. my mouth would water
as she would shoot the breeze. her tales of lands
left behind. made me questions for years
the nature of time. like the red robins that knocked
(on windexed—thrice daily—panels) with no
answers, i too never ceased to try. to understand
each reprimand. we atone as tones persist.

we question as answers resist. like the peculiarity of
liver pate (she'd purchase only from Katz's)
and parrots for pets (echo chambers exist),
cuckoo clocks and misdirected t(r)icks.

in 2022, the weeks surrounding Yom Kippur
coincided with the discovery of a mass
burial site in a ravine in Ukraine. the same
site of massacres during World War II.
and an apology issued by the city
of Philadelphia (several days later yet still
very much fresh—vacuum sealed lyrics
put to the test) for unethical experiments
in 1970s prison kitchens (cells & halls)
on bare skin. the apology dropped
on air, in between commercial bits,

revealed: ### bleeps
concealed: bloops ###

apologies & bruises
long baked / the taste of the sweet
bread and apple cake now stale.
baklava (& backsteps)
often as layered as language

Merriam defines "to atone" as
to make amends or reparation
and acres as physical in nature
skin both a noun and a verb

and i think of recent apologies
formal (the normal) and f(r)amed
& ill times—barely contained

the MOVE bombing
the Starbucks refusing
the statue erecting
the drive-by cruising

empty pails of rock
salt & marrow
buckets full of sorrow
/ all the same

amidst the breaks (predictive
& commercially timed)
the phrase "acres of skin" linger
/ both standards & commandments
defi(n)ed. a hummingbird at the window
(east side) chirps. lyrics of truck drivers
from the north seeking forty acres
to turn their rigs around
sizzle
then settle.
grounds both a goal
& a gully
ravines still fresh
apologies still sullied

of daily tea bags, she'd choose.
chamomile, earl grey, oolong.
hidden behind the flour.
all corners tucked. then
sip from a small cup rimmed
of hummingbird blues & muse

we packed in the middle of the night,
she'd say, as she struggled
to recall the sights

he returned a changed man,
she'd say, as her daughter
struggled to understand

victims of circumstances
& upheaval—a relentless
dance / all skin bare

decades document
travel
as memories stand
still

apologies welcome
but ultimately
an empty attempt
to refill

    # pails on deserted beaches
    # lunchrooms with no m(h)eat
    # evening nursery rhymes that lack a beat
    # migrations (of monarchs and memories) a repetitive feat
    # waters (rough / tough) both literal & figurative

denial / that even a five-year-old
can comprehend

it's been a while
since i've attended services
(too many secular balms to blame)

as I broke fast & consumed
a meal of salted fish (already
feeling freshly guilty for breaking
a resolution to minimize salts
& fats), i read
about the holmesburg
prison experiments
& wondered what
it means to atone

        (## more)

Your Amazon Fresh Order is Out for Delivery – Jen Schneider (she/her)

I spend the break (forty-five minutes) between classes (afternoon and evening) reading. Neither my course texts nor midterm papers, of which there are many. Instead, I sit and wear a hand-knit cardigan (oversized and frayed), plaid skirt, and knee-high boots (faux leather). I'm parked at an undersized desk next to a window in an oversized library. Outside, the season's first flakes dance. One part tango. Two parts waltz. A delayed commute home is guaranteed. I squint, readers (2.5 power) on—tucked behind ears (pierced) adorned in hand-beaded (seed) earrings. I log in (Chromebook always ready) and check for weather updates. My email blinks. *Your Amazon Fresh order is out for delivery.* I check the time. Early afternoon on the west coast. I wonder why she's home. My baby—now grown. I'm neither the consumer nor provider of service experience ratings. I prefer narrow carts in wide aisles. I do not determine order dates. My concerns with doorstep deliveries remain unconveyed. I share the account in name only—my email the designated receiver. My finger pads press. I hesitate, anticipate, click the link. Then look away.

Library doors open and close. The winds whisper catcalls. A student in a navy beanie licks a sour-apple sucker, taps toes, and reads *Hemingway*. A second sleeps in a chair to my left. Another reclines. Eyes on the tiled ceiling. Counting cracks, I surmise. Passersby outside appear distracted. Weather and ice and all things not nice—that's what East Coast winters are made of. I shake off weather-related concerns and focus. Proud of my ability to prioritize. I study the Amazon Fresh order with a breaking news intensity. I scan first, for context and consistency. Feedback routines deeply ingrained. Habits as hard to break as they are to make. I count items and food groups—dairy, meat, grains, greens. My understanding of their myths oddly denied. I review the order as if it's a Power Ball ticket. Seek matches with home-baked favorites. Meatloaf. Brisket. Eggs Benedict. Why, I cannot say. My eyes lift. Outside, a woman in high heels walks slowly. A bandage around her ankle. Wet leaves whirl. A man with a balding head descends a ladder with missing rungs. His work delayed. Locks and luck on (l)edge. A taxi slows then stops. A man exits, then hauls a suitcase up a short flight of steps. House lights go dark. I wonder if he notices.

I return to my Chromebook and confirm accounts (dark webs and hackers lurking) when it's me that watches. The email and its contents, a source of light. A tunnel that connects East and West coast delights (and nights). There is no paper receipt—the kind she'd hold (years ago) while seated in metal shopping carts. Carefully enunciating items. *Potatoes. Progresso. Pastrami. "Why so many Ps,"* she'd ask. I'd shrug, raise eyebrows, and open eyes wide. She'd giggle then continue, *Avocados. Broccoli. Cranberries.* Games of alphabet soup. Each market trip one purchase closer to her cross-country trek progression. I peer at the screen. Regular items on reorder. Grade A eggs. Almond milk. Batteries. Extra-firm Tofu. Diet Sprite. A loaf of Wonder. California raisins. A family pack of chicken breast fillets. *I wonder who she's cooking for*. A carousel of cheeses—Asiago, Brie. Camembert, More ABCs. *Where are the crackers*, I think. Greek yogurt. Size regular. Each of regulars in an irregular world. I think of the times we'd make cheese. A simple mozzarella. Milk sometimes expired. And pasta. Noodles nimble. Mixed then kneaded. We'd stretch arms. Clothes covered in flour. *Take them off*, she'd joke. *It's legal.* I wonder what she'd say to the naked man pushing an empty cart down Broad as spectators whisper. She'd likely sing *Pride.* The man moves with purpose. A blend of seasoned skin and sashay. Sirens follow. Public displays of nudity highly regulated. The library also controlled. Students push past a woman holding *Scrabble*. Letter tiles trail. I spy a trio of As. I think of the AAA batteries on her list. I wonder what electronic expired. The phone buzzes. I jump. It's her. In real time. *Got a sec?* she types. *What's up,* I reply. *Need a recipe. One we'd make. Call now?* I close the device's top cover. *Sure,* I say. Message delivered. Even if there was no time, I'd make it. I grab my Sprite. In good spirits, feeling fresh, I wait for her call. I'll be sure to mention the weather.

Red pin / Jaw wing – Sam Moe (she/they)

It's always *why are you playing with stitches*
in the dim light of the bathroom during Christmas
dinner and never *did you realize sewing needles*
are too big, if you've made it this far, why not try
an electric toothbrush and a bottle of ink, or even
are you brave enough to save your own heart
[not with stitches] but of course you already know
that, you want to know *why*. As in, *why this*
metallic blue eye shadow, why do you assume
you don't look like an angel beneath these blue
tree lights, never *come out to the porch with me*
and *watch while I smoke through a pack of vanilla*
cloves. You're not even nauseous, you're hooking
your thumbs through your belt, lips, your partner
in crime is inside hanging tinsel on a tree your father
cut down from his backyard and drove over in the
middle of the night, if she's anything like the stories
you're already half in love with her, is this why
you're avoiding my eyes, why is it never *light me*
on fire and *Juliet wings look better on you,* instead
all I get is cold shoulder and occasionally, my name
in your mouth. In the kitchen you reach behind
yourself, knowing I'm standing there and waiting for
the soft slip of your hand as you slide a buttered
croissant bite into my fingertips, I have to turn to
hide, bite the insides of my cheeks, is this why they
say the holidays are the loneliest time of the year,
because the person you're supposed to be with has
fallen for someone else, yet what do you do when
they keep tugging at the strings of your apron, or is
it now when I've lost you, and I'm suddenly *not in*
love, just the worst person in this honeycomb-hued
building, you know Frankenstein, you're worse
than the monster, but how would you even know
what kind of creature I am, and isn't this what you
meant, about the stitches? No, you're calling me
a honeybee and clinking glasses with your partner
she is tossing her hair back and sucking down red
wine like there's no tomorrow, you glance my way

and all I think is, *vampire,* not a human stitched
heartstrings in every way imaginable, not someone
begging to be whole, it's *someone who consumes,*
it's *a woman turning into a flock of bats turning into*
the man who climbs around the watchtower, cloak
and heart in one hand, half-melted candle in the
other, do you know what I mean, this isn't about
the lighthouse or the frost biting your cheeks, red
color on your tie, are you picking your nail beds
again, this isn't a haunting thing, please seal me
away behind brick walls and brioche buns, I promise
real good hogfish, no I mean rat, now mule, later
chicken then a gulf of red, Pensacola and mutton,
beautiful bream, knife in the palm but you don't
scream, deli cups full of egg white soldiers, niçoise
and you're flicking smoke over your shoulder
but truly, deeply, unfortunately, it's never *how are*
you doing but *screw your amber ales and pale,*
unloving heart, not *you're holding the needle all*
wrong, you look like the statue of David minus
all those muscles but *you're absurd, and only*
someone with a heart that reckless would care
a dog snaps its jaws, you think *yes, the vermillion.*

NYE – Sam Moe (she/they)

i.

I'm not in love with you. Maybe there will be
mackerel. The evening is amber light and grease,
my nose is bleeding again. You sit next to me in
the laundry room, your back against the bubble
of the washing machine, a crumpled cigarette
between your fingers. What is it with me and
obsessing over smokers. There must be some
kind of metaphor there, I wish I had the strength
to find it.

ii.

It's not that I don't have anything left to give
it's just my heart has worn to bone, in that way
hearts often do, and I'm not sleeping nights. Out
on the porch are our friends, buzzed and shrieking
in the rainstorm. I haven't yet given up hoping
I'll be the one to save my own life. You want to
know why that must be a solo mission. I find I
do not know how to answer you when sober.

iii.

Ribs of velvet and ribbon, the chandelier crystals
half-broken, a nearly emptied bottle of champagne
and I'm eating ice again. We leave the laundry
room, we return with plates of food. No one knows
where to find us. You smoke inside, even though
your ex tells you not to, and of course I'm into
the fact that you don't care. Maybe that's my problem.
Maybe I should try harder.

iv.

When the storm finally stops, everything smells
like lilac and soap bubbles. I'm not in love with you
but I could be, for all the times you've sat by, quiet,
as the two of us deal with the thoughts inside our
heads. Or maybe it will happen when I watch you
later carve out pieces of roast, your hand gripping
the knife, your tattooed knuckles spelling out *hover*
you never told me why you're obsessed with ghosts.

v.

I get it, you don't think I ever tell the truth and that's
a waste of time. It's not about the lying, not really
it's about protection, but you already knew that. It's
about how no one cares—truth or not—I'm exhausted
and I'm running out of muscle. You want to know if
I'll go with you for a walk in the woods, I'm already
grabbing my coat. Maybe I'll figure this all out, but
for now, the water, your cable-knit black sweater, and
your eyes, too-blue, reflecting the next wave of rain.

vi.

Is this about the apple fish?
No.
Baking?
Still no.
And last but not least, crevasse jack.
Dogfish?
From where I stand, green suns.
Heart-shaped mallet, ice burns, jean holes?
Kaluga.
Ladyfish?
The storm is mutating.
Near the doorway, your ex is a shipwreck.
Oven light?
Off.
Promptly, please, eat my heart.

Quietly?
Regardless of the terrible music playing.
Stay near me when we're cooking.
Turmeric?
Yes, of course.
And more ugni blanc, vernaccia, and
when we sit to eat, don't place your
hand on my thigh.
What happened to your heart?
An example of a question to never ask.
Your love is more like a disguise,
anyway.

vii.

The porch is slick and chilly. You want to know
what's going on but I'm focused on flaky pinecones
and gauze-green thicket, I'm into being the villain
too busy obsessing over conch and spotted bonnets,
maybe this is about rose hued murex, I remember
you were all, *quit writing about science babe and tell*
the truth for once but you assume this isn't exactly
what happened, that when we sunk to our knees
in the soft earth you weren't good or graceful, your
heart rewrote itself until your tendons knotted into
a felt thread.

viii.

Can you feel my hands, mycelium rots, did you know
I thrive in decay. This isn't about kissing or killing
or kitchens. This is about details, thorns in brush
patches, gods who are also foxes, a tree you name
Daphne, know I'm sorry I'm a monster, even sorrier
you said you'd love me anyway, as if you know how.
As if you know I'm already on the road to destroying
all this. If you were a god you could save me, or you
could turn me into a plant. After all, why not?

ix.

You're so close to me in the mud, I don't tell you
I'm afraid of blood, these days every doorway looks
like a ghost, someday I'll tell you about the clots.
I wonder where the others have gone. We sit so close,
I could be holding a lamp for you, I could be witchy
and wicked and fun. Tell me where the proper place
is to end all this. That if I leave, you'll be furious, please
be soft, please don't turn me into a jaw.

x.

So, we're in the kitchen again. I can't look anyone
in the eye, I'm burning the pasta on the stove, I carve
a prayer into the cucumber basin, for my body to turn
into a goldfish in a tank, maybe I could be the goat
in the sink, the knife at my back as you playfully ask
for my famous last words, I won't drop the peeler,
I'll be careful, this beautiful lying fling, your mouth is
killing me. I wonder where the water has gone. If we
were never in the storm why am I still covered in peloid.

Places They Never Belonged – Mattie-Bretton Hughes (he/him)

I've lost so much weight.
Chiseled my boy hips into sharp blades,
to starve your heart.
To carve out a way.

I'll hold my breath until I turn blue.
Binding my chest just for you.
But my breasts won't deflate,
and I can't exhale
because if I do, I'll disappear.

My mind disconnects, floats away with autumn.
My body runs away with summer.
And I am her,
but I'm not allowed to be him,
because they'll find out that within this skin
there's a boy who could crush your worst days with that smile.
With the dimple you told her would get her in trouble.

I've lost my value.
Ditching skirts and virtue on the side of the road,
on a cold night where they might
warm someone else's solid heart.

But it won't be me in that body underneath their body.
Just pieces anesthetized, just stoney parts.
My body sleeps with winter.
My mind prays for spring.
When it can be born again.

And unravel the damage they taught her.
To beg not to be touched with too many eyes,
and not to be wronged by so many lies.
And I broke parts of me trying to forget.

How do I become a man now and not lose respect,
for myself?
How can a girl undo centuries of the same repeated sickness?
Shame dies in the sun.
Will the love of the boy within become
a witness?
Can his love bring back all the pieces?

You can't pick and choose which parts you love and don't love about me.
I've already done that for years, you see?
Dissected myself like some cadaver,
fitting my parts together
in places they never belonged.

Womb – Mattie-Bretton Hughes (he/him)

I carry within me
the stars, the sun, and the moon.
A home
within a home.
A whole galaxy.
I can grow miracles.
But my moon turned off its light.
My sun set on the never-ending horizon
And my stars wept and fell from heaven,
when I told them I did not want them.
My body is not a home.
There will be no miracles here.
There is only stardust and ash,
where heaven used to be.

Once Upon A Time – Mattie-Bretton Hughes (he/him)

Once upon a time I lived as a little girl,
and I saw how little girls grew up.
And formed fully voluptuous bodies,
and I looked down and saw
that my small body would become fleshy and full figured.
And my eyes rejected the truth right before them.
And my voice begged my mother to change my destiny.
As if she could move mountains.
As if I could crawl back up inside her
and reconfigure my own DNA.

Once upon a time I lived as a young girl
in a body that grew like an oversized sweater
that itched like a rash,
with burrowing barbs deep inside my flesh,
anchoring into bone.
And I scratched and I scratched
until the light popped through.
Streaming slivers of sun rays.
Until the talons of flesh healed over
smothering the truth.
And the scars formed hills,
and the hills grew too high to see the sun.
Grew too high to climb over
as a hundred hands reached to run over the soft mounds,
as I ran toward the headlands fading from me.
And the flowing red river spilled between my legs.
And I thought that my heart was delivering its grief,
knowing the labor that lay ahead of me.

Once upon a time I lived as a young woman,
and I saw how young women grew up.
And gave their names away.
And surrendered their autonomy.
And disappeared behind grandiose giants.
And I learned that young women,
with their fleshy formed curves
and their wobbling odds and ends,
were to bind and cover these bulbous bends.
Lest they thrill some oversexed giant
and their hundred reaching hands.

And the young woman overheard
The grandiose giant said,
that *the only good woman*
was a woman who jumped in your bed.
And arched her back
like a beast in heat,
and screamed his name
so the gods could hear.
So he could hear
the sound of his own name
echoing off the sides of his grandiose mind.

Once upon a time I lived as a young woman
who was nearly a woman.
Fully ripened and ready for the picking.
And the picking came by a young man
with the same slippery grandiose rant
as the giant that loomed
in the back of my child mind.
His reaching hands pushing me toward the same fate
of the primordial archetype.
And I gave him my womanhood.
And he hung it up like an effigy.
And it took the place of me.
And he exchanged love for vainglory.
And he possessed my body without consent.
And he disappeared until my heart ached.
And he turned his back until my body starved.
And he evaded my words until my mind set fire,
until my flesh caught flame
and burned away any grain of truth.

Once upon a time I lived as a woman
and saw how women became mothers.
Blessed by their ability to perform miracles.
And I knew that my body too,
was blessed with the same miracle as Genesis.
The stars, the sun, and the moon.
They made a home within my home.
A whole galaxy.
But my heart rejected the truth deep inside me,
and I attacked my God-given gift
like a child pillages the tenderly wrapped boxes under the Christmas tree.
And I reached up inside, and I tried
tearing at the woman flesh,
but the flesh would not come free.

Until a young man came inside of me.
And I reached for a bottle but not for a baby.
And I tried drowning heaven in gasoline.
But it overflowed,
and I purged the discernment of my faith.
And I scrubbed my hands for eight hours,
but the blood stains of God mark you forever.
And heaven became hollow.
And my body would not perform these duties,
its God-given chore.
There will be no miracles here.

Once upon a time I lived as a woman
floating around like a puppet on strings.
Living every moment as a given requirement,
to exist in this body.
A body that isn't even mine.
But I have to pay the rent to survive.
and I paid with decorum,
and I paid with modesty,
and I paid with pretense,
and I paid with deceit,
and I paid with regret,
and I paid with silence.
The price of this life is just too steep.
The dark voices keep whispering,
It's time to leave
But instead I hide, instead I retreat.
And I hid as a woman,
and learned not to speak,
and not to be seen,
and not to stare too long at the reflection in the eyes of grandiose men.
Or the man behind the eyes of the reflection in the mirror.
Until one day I stared longer.
And the man in the mirror smiled,
and I smiled back,
And I reached out my hands
and caressed the face
stained with blood, tears, and grief.
And it was the first time a man ever lovingly touched me
with soft gentle safety,
And it was me.

A study on (A)sexuality – Dani Solace (they/he/she)

CW: Graphic discussion of sex

I tried to lie there and take it
like I'm meant to
Tried to like the hands around my throat,
under my clothes, *under my skin*

There is nothing appealing about the tugs on my hair,
the fingers in my mouth, or the cum on my thighs
I'm supposed to like it
why don't I like it?
I swear there's nothing wrong with me I *swear* I'm *trying*
I'm trying I'm

I'm sorry.
I'll be better next time
I hope there isn't a next time

Why anyone would keep going, I'm unsure.
Maybe I'm not built to understand why getting off
is so important
maybe I'm not built for love

If my indifference
is off-putting
I'll never know
None of this will matter
when they're done with me
and I am the hollow angry mess I've always been
and will always be
All I can hope for
is that they don't ask for much
once they've scraped me clean

Is this the price I must pay
to be tolerated?

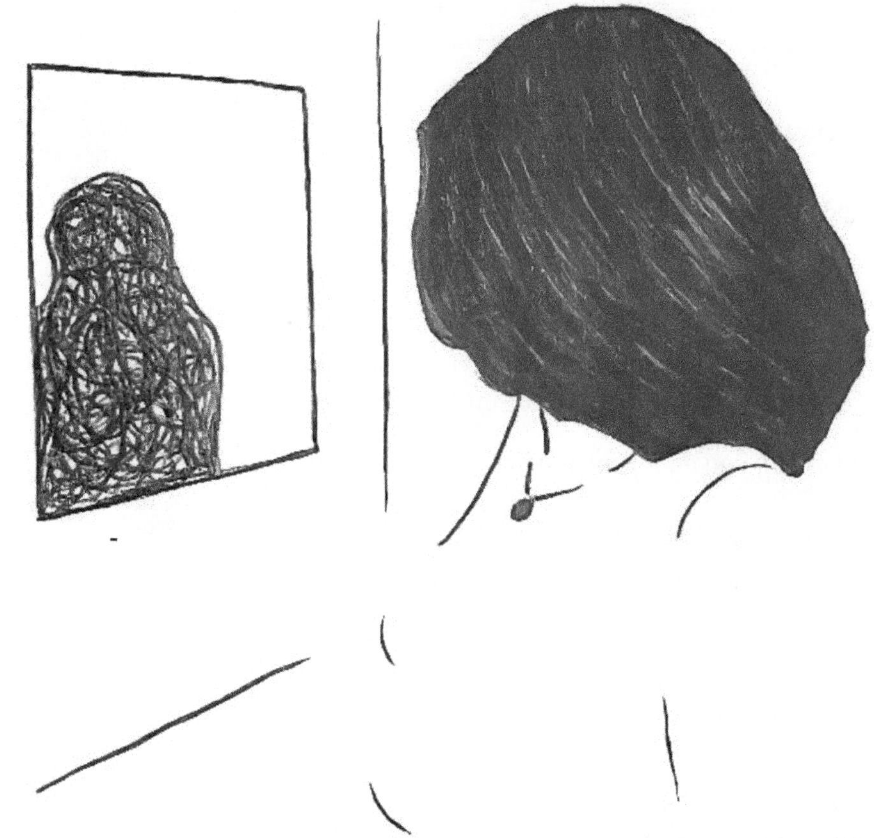

Doppelgänger: Reflecting on Femininity – Dani Solace (they/she/he)
Ink & watercolor on paper

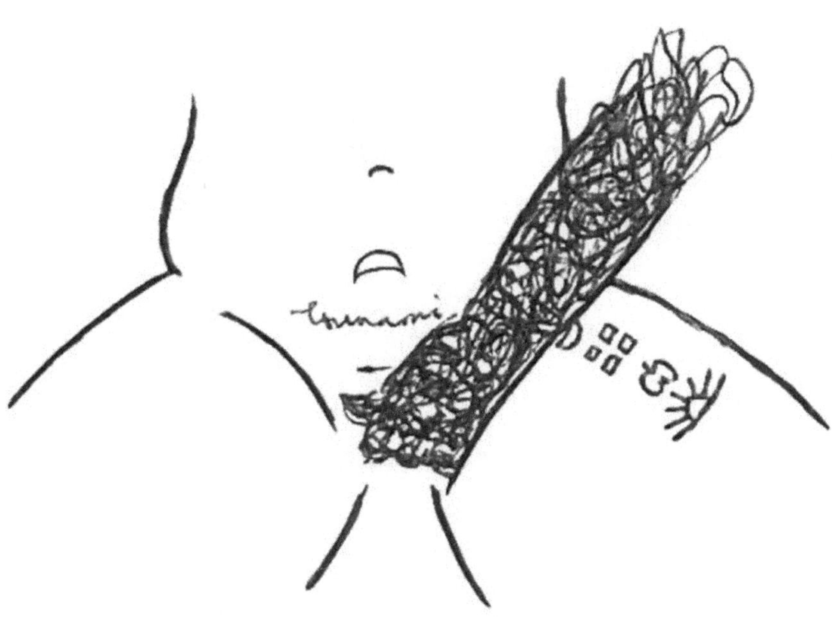

***why don't I like it?* – Dani Solace** (they/she/he)
Ink on paper

Pocket Universe – Jenny Benjamin (she/her)

I crack the seam of my life and escape,

children in tow,

untethered, afraid

cast off into the unknown

What will you do for income?

Heat the house? Keep the house? Feed the kids?

Well-wishers wish charity and feel good about themselves

Do you feel unsafe?

Why don't you ____________?

I go the DIY DHS route because maybe it's my roots

A scrappy people sprouting from coal on both sides

One grandfather shovels coal on a steamship after leaving his Italian mountain home

The other grandfather mines coal in the underground of Indiana, gets killed by a slab of slate

I know how to fill the bellows, keep the fires burning, shovel shit, grind down my spine to

Get there

Get there Get there

The years I call out for years, tick them off in sleepless hours: If I can get them to 10 years,

15 years

20 years

21 years

Don't you even try.

I've been made low, stripped of expectations, pretended misery didn't pound at my ribcage

If my father only knew...

I'm not desirable. I'm not beautiful.

Then why am I talking?

To keep the beauty in the pages. Do you sense my contradictions?

I want to put the stories somewhere, in a pocket universe, a blue world populated with the people who made me

I can slip

out the folded papers when my youngest asks how we got here

I will tell them that I proceed to fill the next movement of my life

with love and more love and more love

Look here, you can be made and unmade

You can sit outside and feel time slur

So what are these stories, anyway?

There's the nitty gritty of the people in my family. Nitty gritty sad stories.

Cancers galore. Severed limbs. No noses.

Blood in the cough, dead upon arrival in Vietnam, dead from fallen airplanes.

Strokes. Prison. Dementia. Brain hemorrhage. Drilled head holes.

Incest rape. Abject poverty.

But also:

Dandelion salad during the Depression. Wine called *Dago Red*, homemade.

There are tubes.

Tubes to drain lung fluid.

Tubes to drain brain fluid.

Tubes for urine.

The wait for bowel movements.

See what I mean? The nitty gritty.

I want to tell you that I intend to fill the next movement of my life

with love and more love and more love

I want to meet someone who I can grow old with

after having love and more love and more love

I will probably die of cancer, despite my efforts to maintain a healthy weight

Live moderately

Exercise daily

Feel joy desperately

I’m primed for the taking: Murphy’s Law

Fat lot of good

What goes up…

I could go on all day

But I will step forward

To the edge

where memory fuses with thoughts

I’m grappling here, grasping for those pure moments

that hold us together

a pocket universe

of love and more love and more love

Late Summer – Jenny Benjamin (she/her)

Love sets down the hard work of the day
and puts away the lunch pail of the past,
as if to say, "Hello, I'm home with you."
Have you seen my misgivings piled at the
doorways of the house? Where are you
putting the smudges and soot that coated
your body like dried blood in the stress-
filled hours of our separation? I keep mine
with the sundry items in a junk drawer:
cheap matchsticks that crack at your touch,
dead batteries I keep from landfills,
scotch tape that smells like Christmas.

Fire wildflowers catch sunlight in this wild
garden. We sit and breathe the air of late
summer. Dusk teases the cardinal back
to the treetops. We vow to watch the bees
each day with their fuzzy wobbles over
thistles and the monarchs with their flashy
wings over the swollen milkweed pods.

Love sits here with us, in the folding chairs,
while I put my feet up on your thigh.
Only the bones can predict what will
happen if we cast them into an array
of language only we understand.

It's sealed between us.

Trans Colors – Jenny Benjamin (she/her)

Living with Ali means accepting color
everywhere

midnight vampire hair dye on the bathroom sink
on the light switch

melted primrose pink crayon in the laundry
on the carpet Jacko-lantern orange soda,

stepped on, an accident, when friends came dressed as ghouls and blood-soaked
scientists on Halloween

boiled flower petals in my saucepan to make watery hues dripping down canvases
the detritus a witchy stew steaming up the kitchen

Upstairs, their room, a collage of colors, dripping pinks and blues and chalk worked down to
dust

Painted walls, doors, wood where colors storm up the ceiling
or serpentine into the tile cracks

My daughter

No

My child

Yes

My baby

Yes

a stream of colors flowing to me
away from me

It's going to be okay.

This or This? – Jenny Benjamin (she/her)

This or This? you ask and that means the fabric tends to rip the skin
starts its meanderings from rivulet to rivulet, gully to gully, this or
this? Wide sky or gray line across a lake stacked like a cake of blues
this or this could be my knee or elbow, clever joints bending beats
say, I can do this or this, I can hold this or this, I can be this or this open
me up one day and you'll see I did this or this with my days because
my organs pulse with life, my cartilage is well-preserved, my hearing
(I've been told) is pediatric, so then how will this body mark time with this
or this? This setting, this time, this place, this fold, this young, this old?
Bring me to a garden, one kind of weedy but thriving with new buds and
worm-run soil, staccato bee movements on the breeze brings me to this
or this sun-soaked day seeping into our bodies or the hazy dripping of night
making its promises of this or this? I can't choose. I don't know which
one, but I know if you tend me, I'll grow.

Dissolving Mothers – Ryan Jafar Artes (she/they)

Like the extra sugar spiking the Kool-Aid,
Extra nip of whisky hidden easily with a splash of ginger ale,
The cigarette smoke that dissolves into cool evenings,
So goes my relationship with my mother.

For at least the second time.
Am I destined for a lifetime of dissolving mothers?
The answer is complicated.
It is, at once, yes, and no.

Complicated by the fact that I am dissolving, too.
On the other side I find a complicated freedom.
One that is dissolving, too.
Everything is dissolving.

<অ-প্রভাবশালী হস্তাক্ষর> *Everything is dissolving.* </অ-প্রভাবশালী হস্তাক্ষর>
The hard part, that has always come easily to me.
Within the sadness find joy.
I know how to mourn the loss of my mother.

I have been doing so my entire life.

I Watch the Roots – Ryan Jafar Artes (she/they)

I propagate my plants and
watch them grow
delighting in the obvious green
though my focus is on the roots
which I watch for and examine
in their clear glass jars
I always allow the roots much more
time to grow than necessary

this morning I popped
a purple trailing vine from itself and
set it in water to grow roots
perhaps hopefully if all goes according to plan
I watch the roots grow
some materialize quickly
others take surprising amounts of time
even different strands of the same plant
evolve at their own pace
in their own ways
once separated

I thought about how I was popped
from my own mother
as I conversed with my plants
about the ever tiring task of growing roots
and yet
we do
myself like the plants
plucking myself from everything I know
until I might find
an appropriate place to grow
roots of my own

The soil conditions
have yet to be those I need to thrive
so I fertilize and water myself
growing into that and what I have always been
like the plants I grow

constantly becoming myself
I only hope my roots might catch in time
to save me
so I might watch myself grow
roots as I watch my plants grow
roots of their own

I wonder how long a human might survive
out of my own water
and soil
away from my family
the nourishment of the sun I was to receive
through the food I was to eat
soaked up by my roots
a lineage
in soil
a family meant to contain me
watered with a language of love
one I no longer speak
by a mother
I might understand

I sing to my mother
as I sing to my plants
knowing they are one in the same
we are one in the same
and the way to find her
is to grow into her
so I might flow back home
into the soil and family in which I belong

Sacrifice – Ryan Jafar Artes (she/they)

I started sacrificing my relationship with myself
on November 19, 1980,
when the couple
who were to become my parents
named me,
Ryan Jafar if a boy,
Lindsay Jamine if a girl,
well before the couple
who were to become my parents
birthed me,
sometime at the beginning of March of 1982,
perhaps between the first and the twelfth of the month,
though such a large, unwieldy, and uncertain expanse of time of
potential birth dates and possible birth times
has wreaked havoc on my life.

My visa was prefiled in November of 1980, too,
and so I was well on my way to the United States of America
long before I was even born in India,
before I was a glimmer in my parents' eyes,
before they even thought their sex might possibly conceive me.

Do not ask me to discern between
which set of parents I might be talking about.
I cannot tell either.

Is there a case in your life when your parents,
who are your parents,
are not your parents?

Is there a case in your life when your parents,
who are not your parents,
are your parents?

Do these questions make sense to you?
Then—and only then—
let's proceed with a conversation.

Do these questions confuse you,
leaving you unable to answer,
because you do not understand what is being asked of you?

Please do more work before possibly approaching me,
and entering into a conversation you have been defining and controlling, the one you know nothing about.

I started sacrificing myself before I ever was and
even knew what, who, and that I was.
I was named with
visa pre-filed before I was
conceived I was
already the child of another family before I was
ever a member of my own I was
separated from my parents before they even had an idea I might be I was never theirs I was
already someone else before I was
ever my own.

I already belonged to someone else
before I belonged to myself I was
already a member of another family before I was
a member of my own I was
already on my way to the United States
well before I ever existed in India.

(A) Female Parent / (Birth) Mother / (Adoptive) Mother / Mother (?) / Mama / Momma / Amma / Mommy / Mom / Ma – Ryan Jafar Artes (she/they)

I am my mother comma
or I have her period

Or comma
perhaps comma
I become open parenthesis
of close parenthesis
her comma
because slash
since slash
meanwhile slash
that slash
otherwise I have never had her period

Instead of being free I want knowledge slash
warmth slash
containers slash
understanding slash
possession open parenthesis
of close parenthesis slash
possibility slash
potential slash
love slash
connection comma
lest I might feel slash
taste slash
hear slash
smell slash
hold slash
know slash
be slash
hug slash
hold slash

cry open parenthesis
to comma
from close parenthesis
the mother I do not know comma
and have never known comma
by becoming her period

When I hold tightly onto open bracket
all that I have ever known to be true close bracket
all I find are lies period

I must let go of even the uncertain certainties comma
which have felt like a semblance of truth comma
though since I have never known what truth is or was comma
I cannot trust even my own understanding slash
knowledge slash
feelings slash
perceptions because of slash
how slash
that slash
the ways in which I have been coerced period

I am missing all sorts of families comma
and I miss the families I am missing comma
and I am not missing the families who are amiss comma
and I am missing so many of my families comma
so many parts of my families comma
the movement of the pieces do not matter comma
whether the families are coming or going comma
I understand them as my own comma
and only when they are going away for the last time comma
can I understand that I do not want comma
or need comma
that which I have never had period

Since all I have known is not knowing comma
discerning my next step is difficult comma
because it is unknown comma
and that is how comma
and why comma
I know I must find it comma
however that may be period

What I am missing is everything I miss comma

and have been missing comma
and so how might I know what it is comma
when I find it open parenthesis
because it is me question mark close parenthesis period

The Girl Is Only Allowed to Have One Story – Ryan Jafar Artes (she/they)

The girl is only allowed to have one story and she is already dead.

The mother and father of my family who purchased me from my family named me on November 19, 1980, a date that only appears retroactively on paper documents in my adoption file, mostly photocopies of the original things, on January 26, 1981, which comes to be an important date in the gathering of my second sibling family, now also dispersed.

On that day in 1980, I was named Ryan Jafar if a boy and Lindsey Jamine if a girl, and so at and by the time I was born perhaps in March of 1982, day unknown or obscured, the girl was not only already dead; she never existed in the second place, though she did in the realm of a first place, one before the realm of usual human existence.

How long might you wait for someone only to find out they are not coming?

How long might you wait for someone before they arrive so they might exist in thought before ever existing in reality?

And so, the girl is only allowed to have one story.

When I look inside, I find her.

I find the girl I never was, the one I have yet to become, the mother I have never met in actuality, the grief in the shape of the mother I have, along with all of the versions of myself.

The container of my body is full.

The girl is only allowed to have one story.

Then why does she have so many?

Kermaphrodit's

NO GENDER POPS

FORTIFIED WITH VITAMINS LGBTQ & VITAMINS QIP2SAA & + & IRON

I CAN PEE STANDED UP !

NON GENDERED AND NO BINARY
GAY FRIENDLY AND MANY MORE
SWEETENED CORN CEREAL
WITH NOT SO ORGANIC
RAINBOW COLORS

NEW

NET WT 1 LB 2 OZ
(18 OZ) (510g)

Cereals – Culkeeen (he/him/his)

artifice: a man-constructed thing – Colette Thalia-Rose Stergios (she/her/they/them)
inspired by lavender by tulips by this morning glory in front of me by breathing by surviving

man seeing man the artificial analog to the natural selection
the survival of the fittest
plant seeing man the part of their nature
the environment the something
to be influenced by their
(generally, ecologically, evolutionarily, slowly)
choices
the flower more beautiful is picked, yes
killed? maybe
more likely planted,
as a squirrel hiding acorns forgets one to tree;
but man feigns control
that we meant to leave some behind.
intention changes not the soil, the leaves
not able to read our minds
how
do we expect
to read theirs?

man being pruned and selected
the artifice choice for His traits
evolving influenced
by those other men round him,
shaped.
does it matter whether they choose their traits
or the environment?
i live in this brain regardless: feeding, responding
choosing
what way i will best survive

how does it fit, then when
my life being trans being
different being
less fit to survive than the
prettier blossom the
more symmetrical the
berry most sweet when
i have
context textures tastes contrasted
conflict in just being in
a world designed to serve
the most behaved

in manner hands – Colette Thalia-Rose Stergios (she/her/they/them)

she in manner hands
writes standing left shivering
cold in the warm room, knowing
what he knew but unsure in going.
standing,
  in joking
    wait tell me
      in joking tone
        tell me tell me
          with shaking hand
            tellme it's not justthe...
              joking tone   hiding the
                tell me   it's   real.
she   in trembling hands
unknowingly sure in body.
she knows   she is certain   she is.

hormones – Colette Thalia-Rose Stergios (she/her/they/them)

i cry more
but, i dance

my smile is the same
but, it comes more

my chest is sore
but i've stopped padding my bras and
i'll have to start wearing
a binder in front of my grandmother
but, i've stopped lying to myself about
who i am

but, i'm living free with who i am

my face and body hair hasn't changed and
maybe it never will
but, i surely see every morning
staring back at me
a woman (with stubble)

a friend asked me
when i started changing
what's new
how does it feel
and
frankly, its hard to
pin
it
down

but, i overheard my dad introducing his kids
they asked oh,
so you have two sons
and two daughters
and he said yes

Tears of the Water – Sam Indigo Lydia Fern (she/they)

Swelling pressure
Surface tension
Four paths diverge, and
I float along the blue confession
-
Release
The Queen of the Lotus stretched down
And bestowed with her left hand a silver chalice
Upon which was written
"Seek not to bring about change
For your presence will carry you along
And the change must come after you"
In her right hand was a rainbow
The elegant mantle of her eye
She rose half from the waves
And she pulled me alongside
-
A winding road whose stones merge from here to end
One stone, One Wheel
Into the body a Motion drops,
And drips a tear into the sea
The promise is Life
The promised is Loss
To give it all up
To the Waters of the Lost
A voyage at hand
To realize desire
Infused with the Land,
The Wind, and the Fire
-
She guides me to the place.
: where all visions meet
I watch the blooming Motion dance.
: in the lights beneath our feet
Images adrift atop the apex.
: a shimmering surface
Of flowers yet unborn.
: wading in this embrace
I glimpse my desire.
: I see the pool it lies in
The rays of the Sun.
: climbing up the horizon

Two souls I know.

: telling of such

A beautiful promise.

: I've yet to touch

-

Beyond that place, we find
The place of wellspring
The Queen's garden of fog
I reach beyond the shroud, my first
Three fingertips break the surface
The first gasp of new life
Holds the trust of the heart
We glide through the garden
Call
"Gather here, joyful souls"
Though the journey has begun
With the truth still untold

-

Four winds disperse the haze, reveal the ways
We might continue
There is respite here
To stay by the shore
Or
There is the haltered breath
Cut short in the icy plunge
"All ways are mine," the Queen reminds me in time
"Shall you stay here,
You shall watch me fade,
You shall feel me slip away"
I sit back and hold the sand, as yet still unhealed
A n d I
D r op it
R e l ax
I a cc ept
I y ie ld

-

Devastating wound
Run through my grip
Trench carved into my gut
Corroded veins
nonetheless
I redirect the flood

A sweeping torrent takes
The palm repels
The treasure cast overboard
Oh ye of fallen head
Know that even here
Gevurah has her say
Drained by the gale
I watch us
Tossed
aside
I watch the sinking chests
And with all that I have left
I close my eyes
I endure
The sobs plunking in my stomach
And I weather the storm
With
out

-
Dispersed tension
A
long
Breath

The
      long
    est
            bre

ath
Percolating golden nostalgia
Two souls I know
Four paths, all hers
In this familiar place I sigh
She holds my head as I float
“Cradle the tender heart,
for it knows not the
changes of time
But only the rhythm”
Release of a yoke so eroding
Dispersed in the youthful laugh
The happiest port in a storm
A free and

familiar vision
-
Cascade of emerald and rose
From the vision pours illuminated images
Malleable mirage, I lose myself in you
Swirling   intoxication
There is respite here
On the last breath   in
I open my eyes
I see the swimming wonders
And I see their rust-scarred lies
The Queen of Eternity lifts high a blurred shape
My body quivers as I recall it in my nape
More
time
here
than I intended
yet
Whisper the flowers,   "your burden is now
Lifted,   a sacrifice most open"
Skin sheened   in sweat
                Submerged   in saturation
                                I must
                            in (passion)|v
                          (desperation)|v
                                (now)|v
-
Emerge
The sky here
Is colder
Droplets,
once crystals of ice,
Thaw on my brow
Seeping
Grasp of illusions gripping
My arms to my sides
Loosened
And I break free
Into another sea
From up here, it all feels so
Alone
The destination nears
Just as I leave it behind
Haste dissolved

In the Eye of Kronos
I list into the tide
I hold her hands
Two
by two
By two
And I leap
-
I land, Elate
silver
prismatic splashing
d vibration from a point beneath my spine
I know this time
When I open my eyes
You'll be there
Lids lifted for
Rising steam
Here I sit
Surrounded by the ones I love
Golden specks flicker through a diamond stream
Dressed in azure lace
I nod my head
And the hand of Yesod draws me
She passes down
the Lunar chalice
The Queen of Life
of Creation
of Motion
Reaches to meet me
Hands joined
We agree
Enter the pool
To forgive
To accept
To love
The rays of Jove
Climbing up the horizon
These souls I know
A beautiful promise
For us to love
So
much
-
Suspended expression

Releases elegance, trailing down
The joy in our dancing spirals
Blends deep
Spectrum twined between her fingers
Hums a resonant light
Patterns of her lips
Reflect through dense water
"It is the most
resilient
fruit who shall be
the one to fall
from this last Tree"
Our dear rainbow swells
A constellation is delivered
In ten stars below
I hold a silver chalice
Upon which is written
"Fear not to live
Fear not to love"
Mantra in hand
And future uncertain
She guides me to the place
Where we will meet again
An everlasting connection
Here at the bottom of our heart
The constellation receives

We   Us
At last
Merge
And pass down
Through the veil
Once more

Vessel – Sam Indigo Lydia Fern (she/they)

All that time,
We weren't doing nothing
The child: the blood of my stomach and the bone of my heart
Asks me
If no vessel holds this moment, how will we not be lost in time?
For the waters erode all bonds,
And the memory will one day release from our resilient love.
For the winds scatter all focus,
And the wisdom will one day slip from our eager reach.
For the soils decay all vitality,
And the strength will one day fade from our vigorous climb.
For the flames dissolve all will,
And the passion will one day fall from our resolute grasp.
If history never knows this day,
Who can say that we ever saw it?
I tell her
You and I
Hold waters in our veins
Memories carried down the stream
Meet us beneath the sea with all who have loved before us
You and I
Share our breath with the wind
Wisdom glowing in our eyes
Dances through the air before all who will learn after us
You and I
Fill vessels born of soil
Strength infused into the land
Creates the bodies of all who move around us
You and I
Act by fire burned within
Passion dispersed as so much smoke
Clears the stalled debris inside all who aspire beyond us
One day far from then
When I pass
Through Middle Sky
Four paths diverge
And I
Remember
You who have gone before me
You who will come after me

Here we pray

And here we honor
Torch-borne guidance
Where we find the ones we love
Four paths diverge,
and
I
follow
you

The B Isn't Silent – Emily Long (they/she)

I inch into the gay bar wearing a nauseam of rainbows,
pin a button to my backpack that yells QUEER! in harlequin hues.
Am I worried the soft butch bartender is handing out scantrons?

Afraid I haven't slept with enough women to pass their test?
The only question on the exam is a 50/50 chance: *Are you ashamed?*
I turn in a blank page & slam the door.

Introduce him as my *partner* or *fiancé*—never *boyfriend*, never *husband*.
Google *bi culture* but can't seem to find any telltale tricks to be visible
for more than one day each September. Already cuff all my jeans

by necessity & have been asking baristas for oat milk for a decade.
Never been to a pride parade. Rsvp'd to the local dyke march
on Facebook, didn't go. Half dyke, half straight as a lightning strike.

When I sit around the dining room table with his family,
I hold hands to pray but keep my eyes open. In 2008
their pastor said gay marriage caused the Big Sur wildfires.

I still have second-degree burns.

I swallow watermelon seeds in the dark and itch to bloom
into something more palatable. Biphobia is the same
as autophobia, by which I mean I am afraid of myself.

When I learned 1 in 2 bisexual people wanted to end
our lives last year—I don't want to tell you which number
I am, but in that moment, I thought I might be real.

I have practiced shrinking so long I can no longer find my speck
of self on the dust-bunnnied bookshelf. I'm playing hide & seek
but no one knows the game has started.

Someone once asked me why I wanted to come out,
their tone more tender than the crushed glass I'd heard
too many times before. I don't know what to say

other than passing is a switchblade: I bleed
in shades of privilege & pain. If it's a blessing to be hidden
& a curse to never be found, then I am blessed & I am cursed.

Forgive me for longing, for excavating an identity
        made of more than *nots* & the knots in my stomach.
Forever searching for hallpasses & permission slips,

        definitions beyond black & white binaries.

Pop quiz:
        Define *queer*. Now define *enough*.
Crawl your way true.

Eleven truths and a lie – Emily Long (they/she)

—After Willa Tellekson-Flash

1. Don't ask me to choose a favorite flower, but it's dahlia season and they look like fireworks without the terror of a gunshot.

2. I know how 5pm July sunlight warms the linen duvet, fills the bedroom—it's honey and I've always had a sweet tooth. I might not know this if depression didn't put me to bed so early. I think I'm glad to know.

3. After 72 sleep-deprived hours with a new puppy, I panicked and almost gave him away.

4. Now I can't fall asleep until his head rests on my thighs, reminding me to exhale.

5. Most days I want to live. This isn't the lie.

6. There's a box under my bed filled with every handwritten letter, birthday wish, foreign postcard I've ever received. I reread them more often than you think.

7. The lightest I've ever been was the day I spent floating in the Adriatic Sea. The same day I stopped believing in God.

8. Maybe it all works out in the end. Maybe we make it.

9. I bought a book called *How To Live When a Loved One Dies*. I didn't find the answer I was looking for, but here I am anyway, living.

10. *Petrichor* also means there's sweetness after grief.

11. I wish I loved myself better when I was younger.

12. My favorite color is now, and wherever we're heading.

When my friend asks me how I know (I'm queer) – Emily Long (they/she)

for Skylar

My 12-year-old nibling just came out as bisexual.
Sky begs their parents for an undercut

and pink hair dye, makes anklets out of pipe cleaners
for every letter of the alphabet mafia.

At their age, I was straight
as a tunnel slide, permanent as pencil.
Brave as a pink pearl eraser. Here I am,

still trying to write myself in ink.
I grow up to stutter at the door of my first lesbian bar,
hide the diamond on my finger I got from a man

who I love and is not all I'm capable of loving.
No one is checking for sapphic references with my ID,
so why does every room look like a worksheet demanding proof

of validity like we did in eighth grade geometry?
Even then, I did not understand why we had to prove
what we already knew to be true.

When my sister asks, voice shaking with fairy wing
farewells and future endings, her child how they know,

Sky replies: I just do.
I exhale an echo that sounds like deliverance.

This preteen miracle, untamable ringlets and maxed-out library cards.
They hate math, and I'm starting to understand.

Maybe we don't need proofs and calculators
and petri dishes. Maybe
we're already real.

A Catalog of Gender Euphoria – Emily Long (they/she)

My first tattoo, a bouquet of all the places I've called home. A reminder I can replant myself anytime a space feels too small. Tie-dye coveralls, indigo softness. Chopping off 8 inches of hair to start fresh in the spring, even when a former friend told me not to. A writing workshop where everyone used they/them pronouns for me and it was helium. Floating belly-up, arms open, in the Pacific, more levity. The snail tattoo crawling down my forearm. Bubblegum pink lipstick. Chunky, dangly, inconvenient earrings. A closet full of shared button-downs, androgynous and colorful and well-loved. Periwinkle nail polish. Tortoise shell glasses and summertime freckles on the bridge of my nose. The picture of me and the dog on the beach, walking toward the wet horizon. We both turn back for a moment before our toes greet the waves again. My languid dress, the color of daffodils, I look like a flower blooming right from the sea.

JoJo Lamboy – AJ Schnettler (they/them)

What does Non/Binary mean?

Non/Binary means revisiting the child in me that never thought of the concept of gender. It means removing all binary concepts of assigned sex at birth and centering rebirthed visions that relate to gender, day by day. It is dying when the sunsets and becoming a newborn when the sun rises. When I think of being non/binary I see all of my trans ancestors, the earth that has made me, the time capsuled places amongst tree and water, and all of the teachers who have helped to reshape my binary conditioning. Non/binary is also a deeper reflection of a big middle finger to white supremacy conditioning that still lives inside me. Being non/binary is my internalized gift of free range to myself and to those who come after me.

-JoJo

Androgyny King – AJ Schnettler (they/them)

~~non-binary means to me, step ste-~~

non-binary means to me, stepping away
from gender norms & being free eternally.
as i continue to learn more about
myself emotionally & physically. I
continue to fight against the gender
construct that was placed on me.
I am taking back my identity
and by doing so i have become
~~ma~~ more confident & proud of
~~myself~~. the person i am becoming.

-Love,
AKing

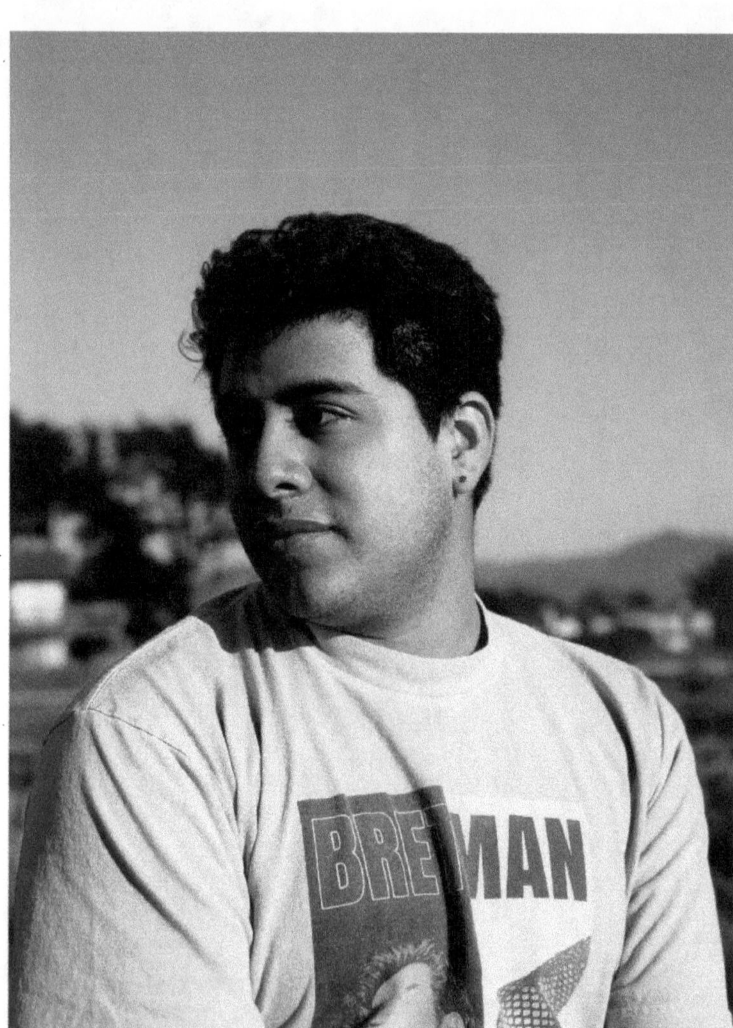

Dei Garcia – AJ Schnettler (they/them)

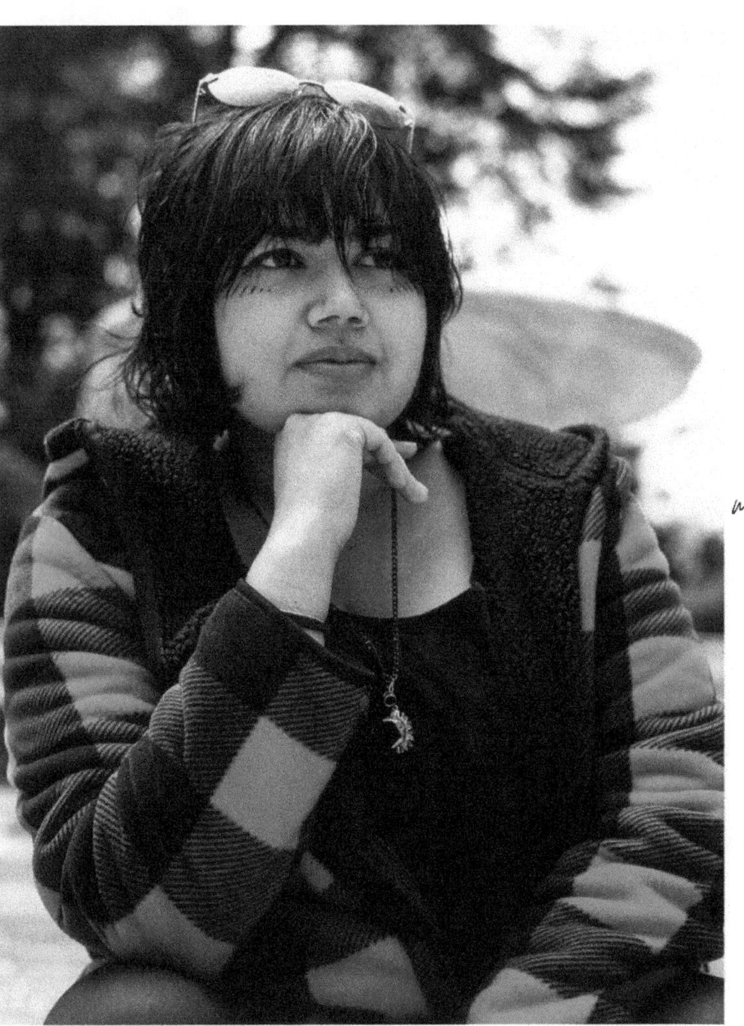

I think I've always known I was non-binary but I didn't know there was a word for it or that it was an actual thing so many people felt at the time. For a while I identified as genderfluid since I felt like sometimes I wanted to do girly / boyish things but as I got older and interacted with both male & female spaces, I didn't feel connected with either of them. I felt much better with the friends that understood me for what I am or by myself. It's hard most of the time since my image doesn't really reflect what I feel on the inside & I've had to become used to or filter out when misgenderings are on a daily basis & that the vast majority of people won't accept me because the concept is so removed from what they know. I've found confort in connecting more with my native roots & finding dear friends who are in the two-spirit community because I'm reminded that these labels & roles we think of when seeing "male" or "female" are just persistent remnants of colonization. I've been lucky to have a family that tries to understand me even if they get a few things wrong sometimes. Being non-binary is rebelling & freeing. It's beautiful & natural.

you+me as angel numbers – nat raum (they/them/theirs)

—After "you+me+everything" by Andrew Daugherty

$2.22

when i have sunk too low, i float upwards
only through words of affirmation and ego trips.
i wail into a velvet sofa cushion, inconsolable
and alone in the candlelight. the next unprompted

kindness you speak resets my
faith's circuit breaker, for now.

⍟555

in the dream, i am never able to touch you.
sometimes i am lucky and don't have to watch
you crane your neck to kiss someone else.
sometimes i don't have to hear her name

or the high notes in her voice.
sometimes my luck runs out.

4:44

i draw closer to you in the cavern of my
chimeras, where the drip of stalactites forms
a shield from the flicker of the northeast
wind through what remains of a flame.

we look the same, but your voice is a man's
and your kiss tastes of sunbeams.

Non-Binary Switch – Violeta Garza (she/they/ella)

they say we were empty,
they say we were ill-fated,
slated to only touch each other   again in the afterlife,
but that in this life, i should never
let you in again. yes. you had me once
and you never will again, not after   the first-rate fissures
on the ground. but we weren't
wrong to give in. it wasn't a mistake
to help you take off your   soft leopard-print undies,
to cuddle on the couch while you
ate your fragrant khao man gai,
to stand on opposite ends   of the room
and dance towards each other.
your tender voice in my ear.
your sternum salt on my tongue.   your wiry body
becoming mine and my unstable curves
becoming yours. it may not have been
fathomable as a long-term relationship,   now that i look
back on the way we mishandled our
boundaries, but what we had—it was
divine and it was sweet. it wasn't a   false love.
                    if it had been,
you wouldn't have cowered when
the parting of the seas projected us to   different borders,
me among the live oak,
you among the pine.

Equator – Violeta Garza (she/they/ella)

0° N

this whole time,
i blamed the end of us
on your cowardice and my vulnerability.

you, upon my exit,
threw out my aromatic spices—relieved, in part.

i, a lonely year later,
collect dirt and hair follicles
under my fingernails
from clawing our root system to dust.

29.4252° N

i have matured into a mapmaker of doors with the softest brush pen of india ink.
never before has this body of mine crossed the equator of her own accord—
away from tender-hearted predators.

-98.4946° W

a little girl watches her
father in ruffles—he glimmers
with delight over her absence.
she promises herself to grow
thorns
and
crowbars
out of her palms.

decades later,
i sexy-walk
into the
automated sprinkler fountain
in front of caladiums and distracted strangers.
my frazzled skirt lifts and my skin jiggles
into the fiercest water pressure in the land.

Future Vigil for a Generational Wound – Violeta Garza (she/they/ella)

It's dark on the water.
In the shifting candlelight,
        I wear the color of ectoplasm
        to the vigil for what has been vanquished.

My mother's ever-present hair ribbons.
My grandmother's single high-heeled shoe in a reddish hue.
My offering of tobacco and song to the land.

All these things
        disperse from my hands
        across the textured ripples, fanning out,
        waving,
        pursuing a different family to haunt perhaps.
On to the next congress.

In life, the women in my family line
        had the resilience
        but not the space or the tools
        to chip away
at their trauma. In death, all their hope rests on me.

They send me dreams of coded weaponry.
I awake with words that are not my own in my throat.
These words
fuse a crystal
of light
to warm our shoulders
across the realms.

After the carnage,
        I breathe out
        without the secrets, the lies,

for once.

Star-Crossed – Marisa Silva-Dunbar (she/her)
—for Afieya

Three years ago, I hid your love letters
so my shame couldn't stare me in the face
each time I opened my nightstand or looked
through old diaries. And now, I long to feel
the soft pages between my fingertips.

You wrote about us spending days at the beach,
wading in the dark cyan of the Atlantic at dusk.
How you wanted to carry your camera with you—
wherever we traveled, capture candid photos of me,

take pictures together in nothing but bedsheets.
You made playlists for every potential adventure
you told me how you imagined driving your car
to my house at night, wondered if I would greet you

in peep-toe pumps and a velvet, red wiggle dress
with your favorite drink in my hand. Dinner
and lust already on the table. We could've played house,
danced bachata in the backyard under the Edison lights.

I was broken then, unable to completely fall for someone
with dreams and a heart that spanned the Milky Way Galaxy.
I wish I could've loved you endlessly like San Junipero,
forever driving off into the golden&coral sunset.

Tempus Aquarius – Stephen Brown (he/him)

My mind has cracks from things that didn't kill me but didn't make me stronger, and there are days I fear falling through, cause when I use my power, I watch them getting longer. If water is emotion, it's a faucet in another room, with a slow, and steady drip. If water's knowledge, it's a bathtub, overfloweth, like muffled voices, coming through, from the space above my crib. I see a drop, now, in my eyes, but instead of falling downward, it travels forward, through the sky, ripples on the clean, clear air, against a shield nobody can see, and for the perfect moment, all are frozen in this land but me.

Mouse Jail – Stephen Brown (he/him)

On the day I was born—the NIH held an experiment on mice, scientists wove the HIV blueprint into every single one of the rodents' cells, to watch how it behaved, then they were afraid of the mice.

The NIH held an experiment on mice. Scientists tucked their pants into their socks, blocked the crevices under the doors, they were afraid of the mice, baiting every deadly trap with cheese.

Scientists tucked their pants into their socks, blocked the crevices under the doors, sealed the air vents, baiting every deadly trap with cheese—on the day *I* was born.

My Sister Eats the World – Stephen Brown (he/him)

Lunar light chaperones, brindled gas giants,
the lush super-earth revolving past a shooting star.

Saucers piled high, dessert centered on clean silver chargers.

The buffet line circles out of sight,
the daily rotation around the crown of her head, eclipsed by a halo

or the camera's flash, blinding those closest to her nature,
as her mouth closes up around them.

Red Dress – Veronica S. (she/her)

M, Murdered
I, Indigenous
S, Stolen
S, Sister
I, Ignored
N, Native
G, Gone

Missing.

My finger drags along each letter of the printed words. They lie before me black, barren, worn, and weary, much like my own heart. It's another missing persons poster, hidden under a flyer for guitar lessons. A siren sound when you live in chaos, a noise you're so used to that it almost goes unnoticed. A simple flyer replaced by another then another until the bulletin board became unseemly. My job for the moment is to take them all down and start over again, fresh and new, like nothing ever happened. No one told me it would be easy, but no one warned me it would be this hard. I thought I'd gotten used to it, like a frog in slowly boiling water. Trauma, tragedy, and constant spilt blood gradually burning me. Yet here and now, this particular page fans at the ember of rage buried deep inside.

Ramona Lisa Wilson.

Her name is printed next to her age, only sixteen. The poster tells of how she was a jokester, played outfield, worked as a dishwasher, and hoped to be the first in her family to go to college. Knowing these things hurt, they cut like a knife—deep, sharp and stinging. But those were not the things that awakened my numb emotions. It was knowing the police had told the family to give it time. They would kick up their boots, treads caked with Native blood, layer upon layer from case after unsolved case. They would laugh and insist this young girl had simply run away. The ugly truth rakes the coals in my belly. Knowing that in the precious moments, minutes then hours, when they could have saved a life, they instead chose inaction.

They chose inaction.

Ramona was a native girl after all. A dandelion growing between the white roses they so carefully cultivate. Nothing but a weed in their eyes. It took eleven months, a breath away from a year, for some unfortunate soul to stumble on her body hidden in the old rugby field. Yellow rope and a nylon cable were her only companions in that forsaken shallow grave. Her clothing was nearby. They never found her shoes.

Where were her shoes?

My fingernails pick at her age, futilely willing the numbers to be larger. Only sixteen, the whole world in front of her. Mistakes she was yet to make, lessons left unlearned, her gift to the world lost along with her shoes. They found her stripped of her dignity and clothes because of inaction, injustice, and being indigenous. I imagine her last horrifying moments. Did she pray someone would help her or did she know, like a rabbit in a snare, that her time was done? She was no longer Ramona Lisa Wilson. Now, she was just another paper tacked up to a piece of wood. I rip the flyer off its plank, my rage burning with bile up in my throat. I want to scream, to cry, to do anything at all. Ramona's dark eyes stare unblinking at me from the paper in my hands. Her mouth forever etched with her lips twitched ever so slightly up in a not-quite-a-smile. Long black hair is piled up mostly on one side, wavy and thick like my own. I tear away at the bulletin board. More missing posters reveal themselves.

Marnie Blanchard, 18. Her remains had to be identified with dental and X-ray records, her body too desecrated to recognize. She entered a stranger's car, hoping for a ride but instead receiving death.

Cecilia Anne Nikal, 15, was last seen walking the highway. Where had she gone? What happened on that fateful road?

They keep going and going. My heart is infected with the poisonous truth stabbing and scraping at me. I gag and wretch, my stomach turning with the vile images and words. These flyers are old, cases I have heard of before, but now that they are here in my hands, hold a new weight to them. The gravity of my sisters' lives reduced to buried and forgotten pieces of paper sends my hands trembling. I crumple the papers, then toss them angrily into the trash. Tears burn up my throat as I quickly retrieve them from the refuse. My feet carry me away from this place. I rush outside.

I can't breathe.

I need to breathe.

The building seems like it's sinking and taking me with it. I run faster and faster to escape its pull. Into the woods, I race until my lungs burn and the tears break through. My body collapses against the closest tree as my sobs overtake me. I stare at the photos through blurry eyes, carefully smoothing out each woman, repairing her face but not her fate. A primal howl erupts from my soul, ripping up my throat and out into the woods. Clutching my knees to my chest and gasping for air through my torment, a voice startles me.

"You wish you could do something?" A woman's voice questions. I nod, unable to look up or speak. "Like all gifts worth having, there will be a price to pay."

"Anything," I choke out through sobs.

"You shall be anywhere they need you at any time they need you. You shall be armed with the weapons of your ancestors and the strength of a hundred warriors." Her words have no meaning. They flow over me as tears stream from my eyes. "You will no longer have a life here and now. You shall become a memory while helping others avoid that very fate." Her words are a riddle I don't have the time or energy to solve. I simply wish to end this cycle of trauma and tragedy. "Do you accept this gift? Will you become Naǧí Lúta?"

A red ghost? My mind swirls with my out of practice Lakota word meanings. My heart knows the answer, regardless. An old native saying echoes in my mind. 'Listen To the Wind, It Talks. Listen to The Silence, It Speaks. Listen To Your Heart, It Knows.'

Even if this voice speaks nonsense, I know the answer pumps through my veins and echoes through time and space. I would be a red ghost, blue specter, gold demigod. Anything to make this stop.

"Yes." I reply, then place my head in my hands. A chill wind rushes past me, pin pricks strike every nerve in my body. My hair stands on end, jolted with electricity. Tingling, then trembling, my hands pulsate on my face. Fear replaces my sorrow. Am I dying? Unsteady hands wipe away more tears from my face, I see no one around but spot a crimson cloak dancing amongst the leaves in the distance. It must be a trick of the mind. My eyes are so heavy now, I close them just for a moment to rest.

I awaken at the sound of my name being called in the distance. Wiping away the dried tears from my face and arms, I force my groggy eyes open.

"Leah!" Yes. That's Jessie calling my name. The thick fog in my brain lifts as I shake the cobwebs loose. How long have I been out here? I glance towards the sky through the trees, but patchwork leaves block my view. I can't tell how much time has passed. My eyes travel to the forest floor where I've left Romona's flyer, along with the others. My instinct is to pick them up, but they seem so peaceful here. This is a better burial than any of them received.

I wave at Jessie and follow him out of the woods without a word. My oldest friend knows me well enough to not push me. "I think I'm gonna go home," I announce when we finally are back in front of the dilapidated rec center. He nods in agreement and I eagerly speed away. I spend my night drifting from one task to the next, a leaf floating with the whims of the wind. Eventually I sleep. Visions of cardinal ghosts, beating drums, and the chanting of my people haunt my dreams. I awaken to the sounds of an April shower in progress outside.

For a moment, everything seems crystal clear. I want to shake off what happened yesterday, but dread creeps in my gut. My eyes open and in my hands lays a red thread. Small strings woven tightly together worries me yet comes with a calmness I didn't expect. It loosely wraps around me before disappearing underneath the door. I sprint to the mirror and spot the thread starting at my chest in the concave hollow of my heart. My fingers twirl around it as I tug on it, a deep reverberation ripples through me, then nothing else happens. I decide to follow it through the house, past the living room and kitchen, before stopping by the front door. I peek out the window as my eyes trace its path to the end of the court and out of view. This is crazy. I rub my eyes, but the thread remains. A quick shower, a cup of coffee, some toast, and it still remains.

Again I feel restless with no escape, a rat in a maze with no end in sight. A deep desire to follow the thread is like a puzzle unsolved. My need to figure it out grows stronger and stronger. Ignoring it, I wash dishes then do laundry. As I sit on the couch, ready to find a show to get lost in, the faint cry of a child wails in the distance. It's not the unbridled cry of a newborn, but the heart wrenching sobs of a toddler. A voice in my head tells me 'follow the thread'. This can't be real. Yet if it is and I stay here doing nothing—inaction when action might help...no, I won't do it. I get out of my pajamas and dressed, a glance in the mirror shows the thread still dangling from my chest over my clothes. I sigh, sure I've gone completely insane now.

Grabbing up my keys, I walk out the door. My eyes follow the thread out of my street to a place unknown. With a frustrated sigh, I close my eyes. When I open them again, I'm in front of a sign that reads 'McIntyre Crescent Apartments'. The crying is louder now, joined by a woman screaming. The thread calls to me from somewhere deep beyond, urging me to follow it until it disappears under an apartment door. I hesitate. I'm at someone's house, a stranger. What if I'm crazy and it's simply a family eating breakfast or a person getting ready for work? What if there's no one at all? I'm about to turn away when there is a loud crash followed by a man shouting.

"Don't kill her!" a child pleads. Panic and rage overtake me as I slam my body full force into the door. It breaks open with a spectacular crash. A tear-stained child hides behind the table in front of me, her fingers rake at her red wrung neck. To my left, a wiry man holds a young woman up off the ground by her throat. Her eyes are glassy with tears, blood vessels racing through her skin like highways and her lips kissed a light blue from lack of oxygen. The man drops her and swivels to me. Every muscle in his body is strained, his face contorted into a manic smile.

"Leave them alone." I command with a strength I wasn't aware I possessed.

"They deserve to die." He replies with menace and venom. His eyes are glazed with hatred, oblivious to the pain and chaos around him. My hand instinctively goes in front of me as a power surges through me. My heart beats to the drumming rhythm of my ancestors, echoing in my ears. My breath is the wind, my blood is rivers running rampant through the land, my body is the Earth turning around the sun—I am nothing and everything all at once. The energy of thousands of people over thousands of years culminates in my heart then spills out through the thread.

The string flows up my hands and transforms into daggers. My body works on autopilot, flicking my wrists and sending the daggers of thread flying towards the man's heart. His body is knocked back, yet no wounds appear. His wild eyes go wide, hands frantically search himself, he holds a spot on his side as if it were putting pressure on a wound, but no blood or gashes appear. In a rage, he charges at me. My fingers clench in a fist and a hatchet made of thick red thread is suddenly in my grip. I swing it at him and it lands squarely in his head with a morbid reverberation. Confusion replaces the anger in his eyes as he drops to his knees. In a moment, the life force has drained from him. I glance over at the young woman. She's caressing her daughter as they both cry. He was going to kill them both. Our gazes meet for a moment, and I see the loss of words struggling in her face.

"Thank you," she chokes out. Sirens in the distance ring as they head this way. I nod and shut my eyes. When I open them again, I'm outside my driveway holding the keys to my car in my hand.

The world swirls around me while my head struggles to keep up. Glancing down at my chest, the thread is gone. Was it a dream? Was any of it real? A million questions buzz in my head, among them are worries that I might have just killed someone. Morality debates will have to wait, though, as exhaustion racks my body. I drag myself back to bed, where sleep quickly overpowers me. I awaken three hours later eager to talk to someone, anyone. I call Jessie. He invites me over for dinner and I'm happy to get my mind off of the chaos of this morning. Yet even surrounded by his wife and kids that are practically family, I still have this sinking in the pit of my stomach. I pick at my food and laugh at his jokes, but half my mind is somewhere else. I keep seeing the man's eyes bulging out of his head, blood vessels splayed in the corner like paint dropped on a canvas. I shake the image away and my attention goes to a television playing in the corner of the room.

A reporter appears in front of an apartment building I immediately recognize.

"Earlier today, a family was saved in this very apartment behind me," the woman announces. I nearly choke on a piece of toast as I inhale while listening to it. Coughing makes my eyes water, but I briskly wipe the tears away, desperate to see more.

"At approximately 10:30 this morning Sheila Faye Kinequon, 25, and her young daughter Christine, 3, were nearly strangled to death. Estranged common-law husband John Joseph Seymour had allegedly had his hands around Sheila's neck, allegedly trying to kill her and her daughter when a mysterious woman broke down her door and rescued the two. When asked about the woman, Sheila said she only remembered a woman in red."

"What's wrong?" Jessie asks as I turn away from the news. There are too many thoughts bouncing around in my head, but the first one to my tongue comes out.

"If you kill a killer, are you now the killer?" He glances at the television and understands my dilemma.

"If someone is hurting someone, they deserve whatever punishment they get."

"But what about the police, our justice system?"

"Is it our justice system or is it theirs?" He brushes his long black braid from his shoulder to his back.

"The Great Spirit has her own justice system. If you kill a killer, you are doing the world a favor. We are not to question the Great Spirit if she calls on us. It would be an honor to answer." He smacks me on the back, and I nod in agreement. "Our people would benefit from having more justice, real justice. Justice like that mother and her child who are alive and not another number in a statistic. A statistic no one cares to acknowledge," he adds, before scooping up his giggling child.

Our people have suffered without justice for so long. My mind drifts back to the pile of missing persons posters. Those girls never had justice, but the mother and daughter I saved today do. I did that. I listen to the sounds of laughter and find a smile tugging at my lips.

The next morning, I wake up refreshed, a little more clear-headed and less crazy. More about the two people I saved is in an article on the front page. I scan down to the part about the dead man, but they don't have many details. It says no weapons were found at the scene. My hand travels up in front of my face so I can inspect it. There are no cuts or bruises, no odd red thread, yet somehow it does feel different. My own body is a hazy reflection in a mirror too far away. Nothing of the red thread or weapons remains, yet the image of crimson daggers is etched in my head. I know I saw them, yet there were no weapons found and I certainly don't have them now. Desperately searching for answers, I drive back to the rec center. My car tires squeal to a stop and I practically fall out of the car, running back into the woods. Branches and brambles rake against my flesh as I frantically search for the place I was before. Part of me is sure I'll see myself there, still sleeping.

Just when I'm sure I'll never find the same tree, I spot it. I can't say how I know it's the one other than a deep belief in the pit of my soul. I would know this tree anywhere. Every notch in its bark, every branch sprouting out, is an extension of myself. My fingers trace the rough bark, searching for answers, but the tree stands stoic and unyielding. I collapse my body against the mighty oak. My heart is a drum beating in my ears. The birds sing the song of my people as I close my eyes.

I'm startled awake by a car door slamming in the distance. I glance down and there, in my chest, is more of a rope than a thread this time. Bright red strings woven together become a network of veins pumping straight out of my chest. All the questions I refused to ask myself earlier come screaming to the surface of my mind. The cardinal feathered rope lies ahead of me, tugging at my soul. In the distance, I hear a woman arguing with a man. I can't make out what they are saying, but there's an urgency in her voice. The rope sits idly in my hands, soft and lustrous. I grasp it, then shut my eyes.

When my eyes open, I find myself in front of a gas station. This place is unfamiliar to me. I'm not even sure what town I'm in. My eyes follow the rope behind the service station to a car. Outside a car two men circle a young woman.

“Come on, we will take you home,” one of the men says with a sneer. The young woman’s eyes are wide with fear, brow creased with worry as she tries to walk away.

“We said we would give you a ride,” a larger man adds before placing his hand on her arm. His friend opens the back door and they push her head down, about to force her in. She struggles, but her much smaller frame is easily overpowered.

“No. I don’t want to go with you!” No one else is around to notice her fear or listen to her cries for help. On this side of the station, the building hides them from passing cars and prying eyes. Even the attendant is safely inside, where he can not hear her. A fury builds inside me as I rush to her aide. The rope slides along my outstretched hand to my balled fist. It molds into a long spear, complete with a feather decorating the hilt. The tips of my fingers sense the subtle grains won from many battles before. I take aim at the larger man’s heart while the smaller one tries to push the young girl into the backseat. The spearhead pierces his chest, his body arches as if impaled, yet no wound in his body or tear in his clothes appears. The other man releases the girl and charges at me, his fists flying. His efforts hit me like the playful tapping of a friend. Out of my hand comes a large, furry claw. I swipe across his chest and he stumbles back, crying in pain. He collapses to the floor, freeing the young girl from her captivity in the back seat. Her tear-stained face eyes me cautiously, then she hops over the man on the floor fleeing towards the store. The young man looks up at me, eyes wide with fear. I could rip out his heart. He deserves it.

It’s justice after all, isn’t it?

A tear pools out of the corner of his eye and for a moment I notice how young he is, perhaps eighteen or nineteen, still just a babe wandering around on wobbly legs. I lean my face dangerously close as a whimper escapes his lips. I whisper in his ear, “Don’t let there be a next time.” In slow steps, I gradually back away. With the rope firmly grasped in my hand, I squeeze my eyes shut, wishing myself away from this place.

My eyes flutter open and I’m back at my tree. The rope now vanished, leaving me weak and alone. I am a shadow of my former self. Every bone and muscle in my body is hazy and uncertain. This gift—or curse eats away at my human self a little more every time I fall asleep and wake once more.

What have I become?

The question lingers, festering in my mind until heavy eyelids and a weary body give way to sleep once more. I wake up in a cold sweat. For a moment, I’m unsure where I am. Am I saving someone or killing someone? My body is shaking, my soul rocked to its core. Displaced, fuzzy thoughts swirl. Nausea bubbles in my stomach, threatening to overwhelm me. Unsteady legs walk me out of the woods to the rec center decorated with pumpkins for Halloween. It was April only a moment ago. The light is on, so I make my way inside. Strangers mill around. No one pays me any attention. I am but a ghost haunting these halls. I make my way to the archive of news and search until I find it.

The picture of the gas station is what draws me in and the sentence keeps me here. "Lana Derrick, 19, says two men tried to abduct her when a woman in red saved her life." She would have been lost. Like so many others—too many others. Everything is in a haze as I head back to my tree. I slide against its bark and lean into its trunk. "I don't know if this is right. Am I a savior or a villain?" I ask the leaves and brush, they do not answer. My eyes close for a moment until the sound of a loading shotgun rings in my ears. I open my eyes to dewy grass, the sound of birds and a bright display of colored flowers at my feet. Warm sunshine on my face tells me it's not fall anymore. My eyes go to my chest where a red ribbon is now protruding. As it grows, it encompasses me more. A man's voice is screaming, cocking a gun in my ear. I understand now what I must do. My eyes snap shut, then open again.

Bulky, sloppy, and crass, the man stands before me. He holds a sawed-off shotgun pointed at a woman's head. I rush into the small house, no one aware of my presence. The demon of a man stands before me, the hatred in his eyes burns like an inferno. The ribbon snakes up my arm, then turns into a bow and arrow. Without hesitation, I pull back and let the arrow fly towards the man's heart. He stumbles back then lunges forward, spit frothing at his mouth. Then the ribbon is an axe. I aim at his head. The sound echoes through the house, a terrible sickening thud as his body hits the floor. I glance back and see the woman holding a younger girl, with long scrawny arms and big, brown, indigenous eyes. She reminds me of Jessie's daughter, who is only twelve. They caress each other and cry. My sisters—a daughter who might have lost her mother, a mother who almost lost her daughter. They are strangers in every sense of the word, yet I feel as if I know them better than myself. They are me.

"Thank you, thank you," the mother says, her voice muffled by tears and her daughter's dark hair. I nod, then close my eyes, ready to return to my tree.

For a few sacred moments, I fight the heavy sleep tugging at my eyes. I drift through the woods back to the rec center once more. Once upon a time, this was my only home. I drift back to the fateful cork board. Now it's decorated in neon pinks, oranges, and yellows. Celebrating town events, announcing neighborhood parties, things this city had been afraid to do for so long. A few even featured a lone red dress and the words thank you drawn with children's hands. Only one missing poster remains on the board that was once saturated with them. It is my picture from Jessie's last birthday when I played with his daughter. I have a wide smile, my black hair piled to the side, a bright red dress draped over my body. I miss my friend. Guilt for the heartbreak he must have gone through after my disappearance gnaws at me. Seeing this flyer now, I know what I must do. I grab a pen on the table nearby and write, 'The Great Spirit has called on me. I have answered.' This is my last will and testament. Jessie and his family are the only ties I have to this world. He will recognize my writing. He must know in his heart this is what I must do. One poster to replace a dozen is a trade I would make any day and will make over and over until the Great Spirit calls me home. The question of justice is not mine to answer, I am but the blunt instrument tasked with its purpose.

I am finally at peace with who I am and what I am. The Sacred Earth has chosen me to be the one to deliver justice for my sisters who have been stolen and savior to those who refuse to disappear. The woods have become my home now. My red ribbon has grown into a rose colored cloth. Patchwork thread winds together tighter and longer with each life I save. The threads are my sisters, each stitch a hope and a dream, each knot a hand extended, holding onto the one next to it. The cloth becomes a dress which becomes my sigil. For years to come, those who would harbor ill intentions will hesitate before acting out those horrendous deeds. I no longer shed tears for those who hunt my sisters. They are murderers, mutilators, violators of our sacred hearts.

The spirit that spoke to me that day told me the gift of saving lives would come at a cost. I realize now as I lay my head against the mighty tree that this is exactly what I wished for. Maybe this has always been my fate, and for that, I am grateful. The screams and pleas for help will no longer be ignored. Those with evil festering in their hearts fear me, they fear the Naǧí Lúta or, as the people have come to call me, the "Red Dress." I am a red thread woven into a ribbon, bound into a dress, carried in the wind.

I am ready and waiting to save my sisters—those who will not be stolen any longer, who deserve to exist.

Untitled – Victoria Johnson (she/her)

On Church Grounds – Isabelle Quilty (she/they)

The foundation remains
Where wax-dipped fingers once repaired flesh and bone
They pressed idols into our hearts with hymns and the flavoured tongues of heretics
Bloodied lips
Chipped teeth
My skin is waxy now, painted with the stick-and-poke
Existence cradled in lucid dreams
To taste the body is to see God in places least expected
The moths are drawn to me
Mother to skin
Skin of the teeth
Pain supplemented with lamentations
A graveyard bound in Irises
I'm not prithee to the ways of men
The ruin that flickers in their wake
I am mud and ichor
A creature of abyss and lust
My skeleton was buried between granite and earth
Forgotten by the preacher
Baptised by spittle and the salivation that draws all men
I'm roused from the dream with a black spine
Leathery, mottled wings stretch wide to greet the night
The choir embraces me with hands cold with sweat
Broken by a fever
A stupor that strikes them right down to the soul
They will hold their saints close to their chest
When I darken the skies

Star Fire Rising – Madalyn R. Lovejoy (she/they)

Through avenues of expression,
I both delight and discomfort
An uneasy presentation
Falling somewhere along the line
Of what is and is not acceptable

When embodiment feels alight,
I revel in the weirdness
An eternal star fire rising
Singing from the joy and terror of dealing
Piercing damage with my wondrous form

A Queer Memory – Madalyn R. Lovejoy (she/they)

I remember being asked out in fourth grade—not by the kid, but from his friend. When I asked him why, he said, "You are caring, responsible, and you seem like you can cook." I remember thinking that that was a strange reason to ask someone out at eight years old, but despite the Freudian tendencies, he wasn't wrong. I do emanate a warm energy and cultivate calm, but I knew even then that my tender heat would never burn for him. Not for one of his kind, his mind, his might. His careful consideration meant nothing, his idea of a mother-wife not the life for me.

Of Critical Cat Calls – Madalyn R. Lovejoy (she/they)

The careful plan put into place
To lurk, and stalk, and watch, and terrify
All from the safety of your own car

With the comfortable crew
Piled into your jacked-up Jeep
You leer out the windows, faces gaping
Mouth-breathing for any reaction
From those passing by

Oh, the utter masculinity of a ride
With led lights on the frame
A glaring beacon for the horrible
To excise their misplaced power,
Onto passerby previously in peace

Tuesdays with the Ghost – LindaAnn LoSchiavo (she/her)

Some rituals might be afraid to die.

You're *here* allowing emptiness to do
Doom's work, reminding me emotions, rage,
Regrets continue in the afterlife,
Kinship's bond scarred like walls where family
Portraits, removed, left ugly holes behind.

Your shoulder shrug's suspicious silhouette—
Felled untried wings—had been inherited
From grandpa, whose Aeolian nature
Had cultivated fortitude, aware
Volcanic force can be a ruinous god.

Some rituals, like Sicily, run dry.

Inviting death to a staring contest, you
Assumed the posture of a guillotine,
Betting against the beauty of your life,
Daring it to expire—or to apply
A tourniquet, compress pain's blood-red rain.

Our weekly ritual survived, stood by.

We'd meet for lunch on Tuesdays, holding hands
En route, which calmed you after therapy,
New York's vehicular va-room our song.

During one meal, amid those chin-cupped sighs,
Forlornness wrote dark scripture down your back.

You'd just seen Mauna Loa's volcano.
A flirty guide lured you to the gift shop.
With his communion on your lips, you bought
A hideous Hawaiian souvenir,
You're cursed to wear in perpetuity.

Cute hula girl, displayed on red shantung,
Saluting tiki gods, mid-dance, alone:
Was she your last embrace, strained neck tied, noosed,
As hula girl surveyed the upturned chair?

You did not call me on your way to ash
As angst unbuttoned from the terrified
Fist your heart had become, swung loose, released.

Today is Tuesday—but no lunch is served.
You can't escape woe's blacked-out page because
My memory's the urn I'll store you in.

–

Joseph LoSchiavo, who ended his life in 1977, is buried in Green-Wood Cemetery, Brooklyn, NY.

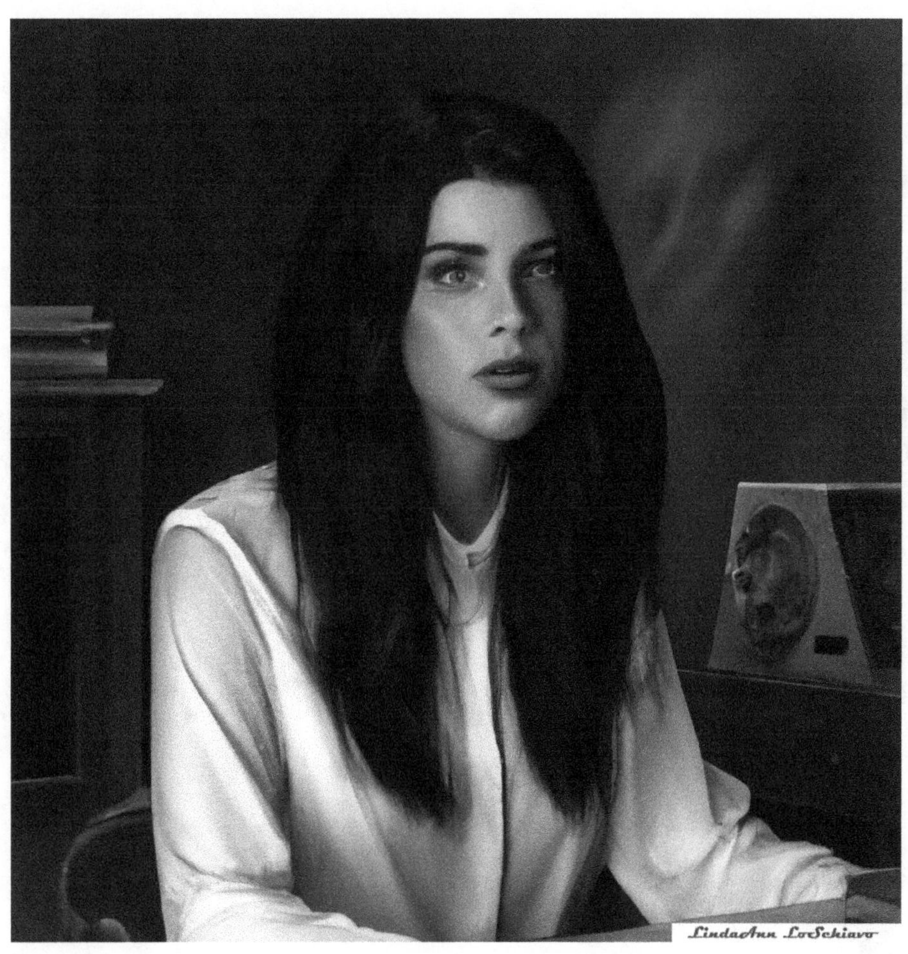

I am here – Lee Martínez Soto (they/them/ellx)

"Transsexual. It's when a woman wants to be a man."
Corrected on my own sense of self,
my previous words erased
by outdated terms that could only come out
of the ashen lips of a dinosaur
who should have retired many centuries ago.

He asked, "What does your husband think? Won't he miss...?"
hands squeezing the air between them and his chest,
the only eye contact I had through the session
happening as he mimed hands groping breasts.

I sighed in all the stages of grief
and landed on disbelief.
I shook my head no and reassured him again
with a, "I can bring him in if you want to.
He's waiting for me outside."

Head shaking,
pen scratching against a yellow notepad,
"I will have to diagnose you.
A test, some sessions, then
I can make a recommendation."

I thought, "I was not aware I was sick."
I said, "would that help with getting my surgery?".
I thought again, "Why should I ask for permission?"

Therapy, then maybe hormones, then maybe
after a few sessions of me paying him
to tell me what I had already explained,
surgery.

He ushered me through the door,
impatiently handing a note to his secretary
and murmuring,
"Set HER up for an MMPI for next week."
He disappeared behind the closed door of his office,
where I had told him my illegal name,
my undocumented pronouns,
my body's immigration goals.

I thought, “THEM.” Capital letters, full stop.

Meanwhile, the secretary called me by a name
I had buried 6 feet below ground ages ago,
while looking at my paperwork with my illegal name
clearly written across the “preferred name” option that
apparently was only there for decoration.

I thought, “Lee.” One syllable, ambiguous, mine.

I said nothing.

“You won’t see him that day; it’s just an exam, 3 hours. Bring
some water.”
I said I would call at a later time to schedule it,
instead of ignoring her deadname me
and misgender me for the sixth fucking time of our interaction.

I hung up the phone on her days after
when she called asking for “Deadname”,
informing her of a copay,
I said, “I don’t know her.”

Repeat this exact experience
only I have wasted months with him,
his performative allyship apparent only
when he talked about friends
that gave no permission
for him to disclose their lives
and out them to a total stranger.

I thought, “Will he ever shut up?”
I nodded and tried to interject here and there,
interrupted by his complaining "Oh, all those made-up labels." and
comparisons of the collective us to child predators
infiltrating our already vulnerable cultures.

I thought, "Oh, fuck no."
and tried to correct him.
He gave me two books
and sent me home to find other ways to cope with
dysphoria,

stop astral projecting out of this meat prison,
and maybe distract me from finding
made up words to define me.

He called months after,
after he realized he missed
those 30 bucks a week I had added to his budget.

I let it go through voicemail,
deleted;
left him on read,
deleted;
then blocked.

Wasted my years from 22 to 32
trying to find me and end me,
a decade worth of the same ol' same ol'
where I learned to hide myself from specialists,
a care team that I should have been able to trust.

Yet still being out and about
in the company of my hairstylist,
piercer,
tattoo artist,
and strangely, ob-gyn
who showed more empathy
than any other paid piece of shit therapist,
psychiatrist, social worker
ever did.

I thought, "This is now on my terms."
and I said it out loud,
too fed up already to pretend.

I thought, "Well if following these rules has only postponed
my transmutation 10 years,
might as well use these anchors
tethering me across borders
to falsify the anguish,
to make it just strong enough
to be alarming."

"What's one more anchor baby
doctor-shopping across the border?"

I asked of them
to circumvent the insurance policies,
made accomplices of the empathetic people
who had made unsafe places feel safe,
even welcoming.

I said my name,
my pronouns,
my transition goals;
they justified procedures with minor circumstances
so that I could live
and just
be.

I am here
and I'm not going anywhere.

For those not on the know
my name is Lee Martínez Soto,
roll your Rs, get the acento right,
don't come at me with your gringo version
because you can't be bothered to learn.

I break the boundaries of the binary,
I am gender chaos,
gender unknown,
gender 404 not found.
My pronouns are not optional,
plural they because the singular
cannot encompass the vastness of me.

Dear Cis People: – Lee Martínez Soto (they/them/ellx)

Repeat after me,
"My pronouns are not
preferred,
optional,
an alternative
for you to ignore
overlook
change
when you don't feel like
believing me about who I am,
when you don't really care for
respecting
acknowledging
my existence,
when we argue
and you seek a surefire way
to shake me to my core."

Dear Cis People:

It's been years
since you last opened
let alone read
any biology books,
peer-reviewed journals,
or even read or listened
to the emotional labor
that I and many others
have screamed and cried
at the top of our fucked-up lungs.

"Biological gender"
is as wide and varied
as your excuses for why
you pick and choose the words of a god not ours
to abandon scared and lonesome children,
gatekeep life's basic experiences,
and shock us into casting away
who we are.

Don't you think it's
a little creepy

to change your opinion
about who I tell you I am
based on your own assumptions?
Like, why are you so obsessed with me
and with what I hide under my shirt
under my pants
between my legs
tangled on these vocal cords?

Don't you think it's
a bit disturbing?

Dear Cis People:

If I say
my pronouns are they/them
my gender is chaotic neutral,
the essence of that power trip
of the fear that crosses bigoted asshole's faces when
they see me stomping
on these platform boots
and torn up tights
paired up with high-waisted shorts
tight crop tops
these tattoos
pierced face
green hair
shaved sides
(oh, the euphoria),
that is exactly what I mean;
this is not an invitation
for debating
questioning
or shoving
your poorly informed beliefs
my way.

Dear Cis People:

My gender is not
a personal attack
on you,
but please do take
this hereby letter personally.

This is
about you;
you know your names,
your multiple slips
that I will no longer pretend
are mistakes,
your pretense at allyship,
hollow empathy,
sympathy,
followed by your barrage
of endless
deadnaming
misgendering
and passive aggressive
bullshit jabs
that do nothing but chip away
at
this
already thin
patience.

So here's the end of it,
Dear Cis People.
I will now meet you at your level,
stomp straight to the ground
where you scurry away,
like pestering little cockroaches.

Dear Cis People:

Fuck around
and find out.

All Women Are a Mother's Daughter – Lucy Puopolo (she/her)

CW: eating disorder

By the time she's old enough to know that she should care, Thalia has already grown accustomed to hacking the ever-present post-cigarette phlegm out of her windpipe. She spits on her lawn, which is just the sad patch of straw-colored grass in front of her trailer. Sorry, *mobile home*. Denise hated the word "trailer."

Thalia had always found it pathetic how her mother liked to pretend they were more than they were, how she would hiss "*mobile home*" before sucking a deep inhale from her sixth finger.

She had once told Denise that all the pretty rich women snort coke now. It's classier than cigarettes, more feminine to consume your sadness and not leave a mess than to take up space with smoky exhales.

She raises the soda can to her lips.

Diet Coke always leaves a film in her mouth, that fake sweetener aftertaste she can't quite wash down. The sticky metal tab smells like standing on the toilet in a too-small bathroom to see her full body in the mirror, pinching at the way her belly perched on the waistband of her jeans. The bubbles whispering inside the can are microcosms of her mother's cheap rings rapping against the flimsy door, punctuating her shouts about having to pee, so get out of there already.

Diet Coke tastes like the entrails of the promise she made to herself too many years ago, the promise that one day, her mother and this *mobile home* would be nothing but a story people didn't believe was about her.

All the liquor store magazines praise a pop star's quickly-slimming figure. There's something vaguely animalistic about the neon yellow block letters that read, *The Bonier the Better!* Thalia stares into the mirror above the sunglasses section and realizes why she is worse.

But she was nothing if not determined. She decided that one day, she would be on magazines, and show all the girls who bought their jewelry from the drugstore that they, too, could go somewhere in life. She would convince all the girls that lingered too long at storefront windows that they, too, could become something more.

But to do that, she had to get better.

So when she saw the kids with their thrift shop t-shirts around the park, she'd make sure to slip a compliment through her yellowed front teeth. She would be kind with herself those nights, clipping her fingernails before reaching for the back of her throat. She started saving all the loose change she found on the ground, keeping it all in a shoebox in her underwear drawer. Pounds fell off of her, taking with them her girlhood, too soft to be bone. She had to be bone.

One night, she confessed the dream to her mother, pressed up against her chest while they watched a gameshow on the bulging midsection of their television. She had whispered when she said it, her words made of glass.

Denise had laughed, popping lungs smothered by layers of flesh.

"What's so funny?" Thalia had asked. A horrible feeling dropped into her aching, tender stomach.

"Oh, Jesus, Thalia, get serious," Denise had chuckled. "Girls like you and I don't go anywhere."

Thalia didn't want to believe her at first. She told herself that she was not in the same category as her mother, who only left the trailer park a couple times a week and never washed her face. She was not hopeless, she was not lost, she was not going to give up on herself and her dreams. The word mother left her like a curse.

Thalia now wonders how old Denise was when someone fed her that same sentence. She wonders how long it took for the words to dissolve into her blood like sugar into hot water, thickening until her body was too heavy to bear.

A week after that night, Thalia took the change box out from her underwear drawer. She walked down to the drugstore, cardboard box sagging in her hands like a teardrop, and bought her first pack of cigarettes. The cashier just handed them to her. He didn't ask questions. He knew what she was.

She wonders if one day, she'll say those words to another little girl and watch her face crumble like an empty Diet Coke can crushed under a heel.

With an exhale of smoke, she leans back in the lawn chair and lets the sun seep into her tired skin.

Thalia was angry for a long time. Too long. So long, in fact, that it wasn't until after her mother had been lowered into the ground under her childhood magnolia tree that Thalia realized Denise, too, was once a girl with a dream.

It wasn't until she was cleaning out their *mobile home* that she found a stack of tabloids under her mother's pull-out couch bed. Later, curled up in the springy, lumpy mattress, hugging the magazines like a lover, hot tears carving rivers into her cheeks, Thalia wondered why she never told her mother she was beautiful.

Because she was. Oh, God, she was.

Thalia wishes too late, as all wishes are, that she could apologize to her mother. She wishes she had painted her mother's nails with the fancy polish they never splurged on and asked her what she wanted to be when she grew up. She wishes they had spoken, just once, like the girls they never got to be, instead of the women they were forced to become.

She realizes now, facing the sun, proudly burning, turning a furious, ugly shade of pink, that she *is* like her mother. And for the first time in her life, it sounds like a blessing.

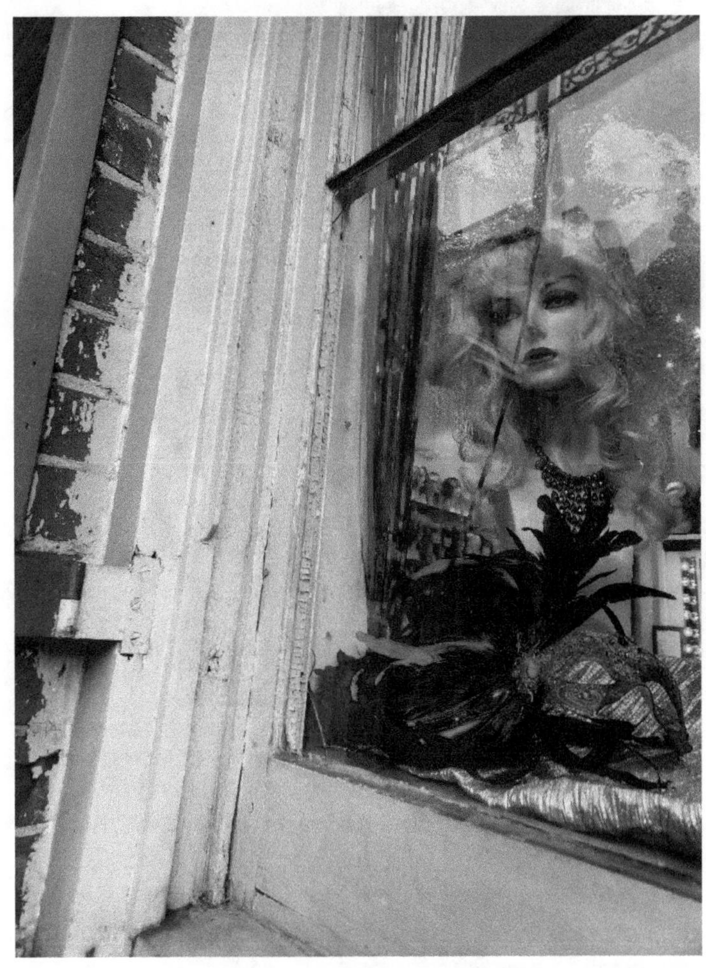

doll – Abigail Guidry (she/her)

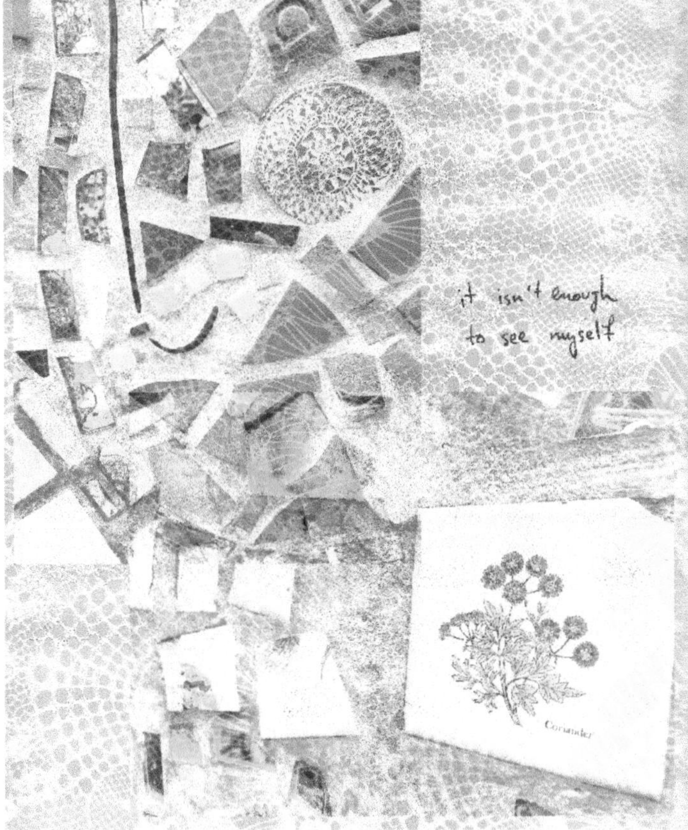
it isn't enough
to see myself
Coriander

enough – Abigail Guidry (she/her)

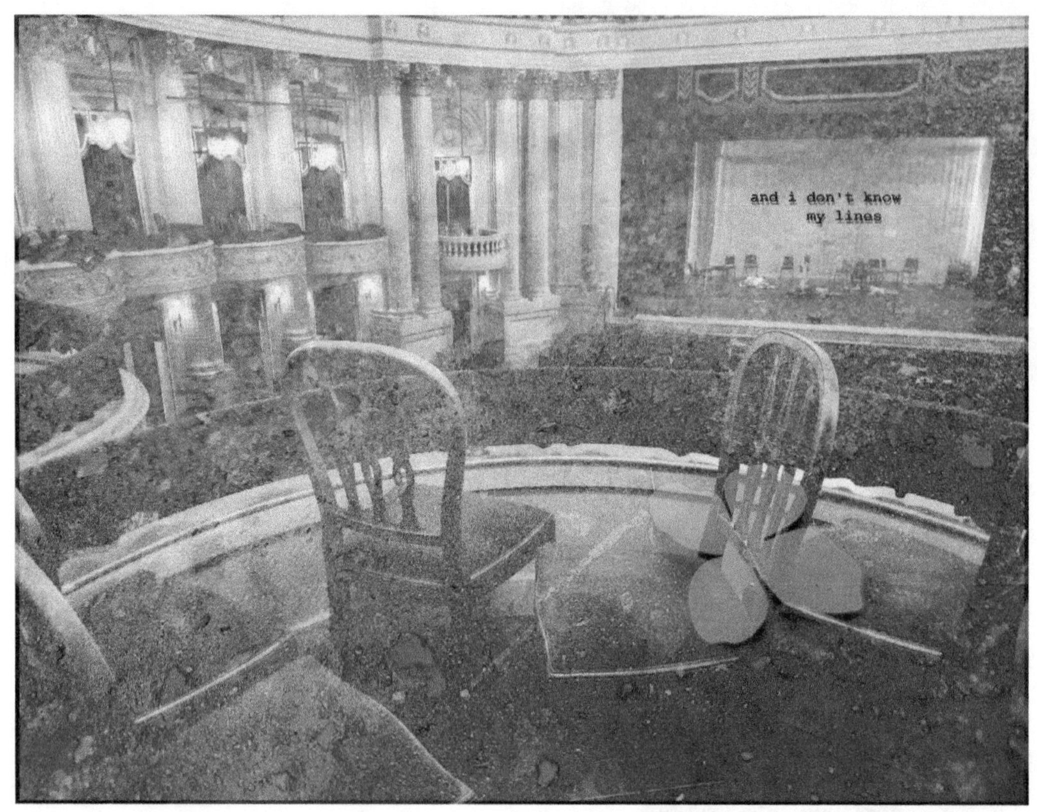

performance – Abigail Guidry (she/her)

scratch – Abigail Guidry (she/her)

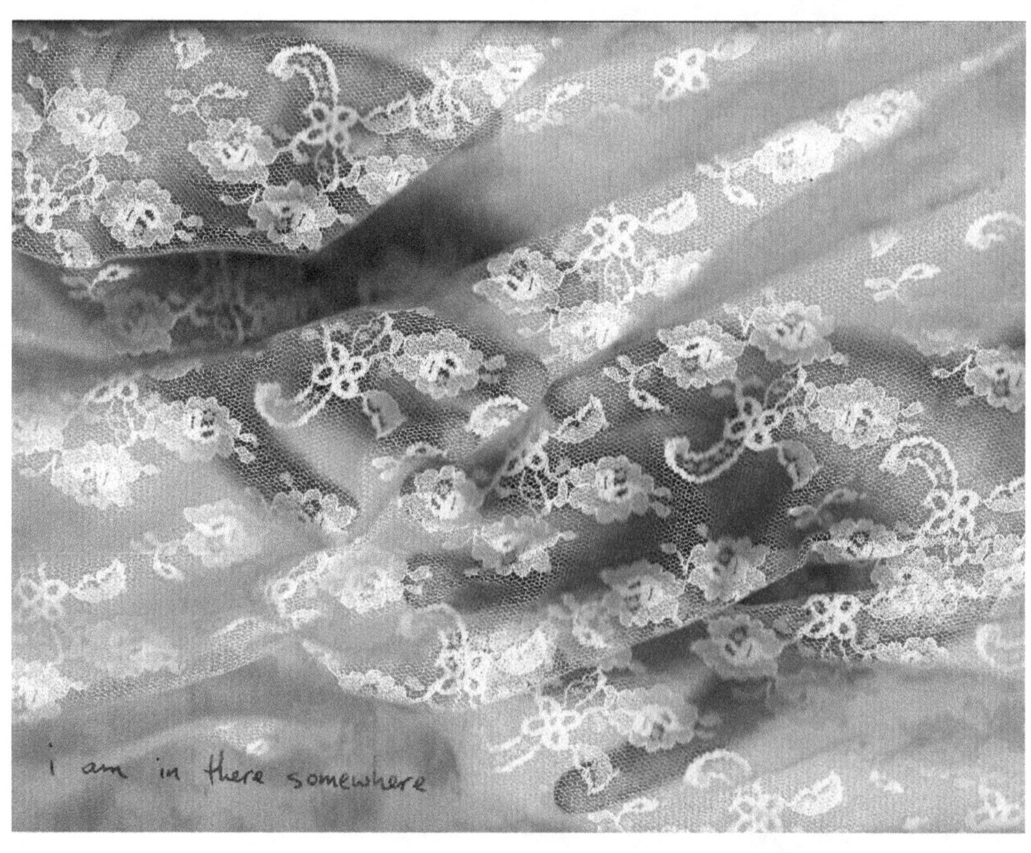

The Burden of Blood – Shelley Sanders-Gregg (she/her)

I observe the lady at the check out line and
wonder if she feels it, too
with her perfectly manicured nails, crimson red

NO blood red
like the vials they draw (or, rather, drain), repeatedly
in vain (by vein after vein) in an attempt to
decipher the abhorrent enigma
inhabiting my body

or the stains on my panties when I realized my first child
would never live in this world

or the monthly reminder that I am strong enough to bear it all

all the while, coming apart at the seams

I never wanted to be the reason he doesn't sleep at night,
flopping like a fish out of water,
hoping for a breath of air,
we're both gasping for a s i n g l e breath of air
to get through this f u c k i n g mess.

And the angels that live inside these walls,
disguised as children,
feed me, unknowingly.
I would have starved to death long ago
without their nourishment.

But, I... I chew on my guilt, like cud, for so long
it gets stuck in my throat
as I gag on the awareness that I'm both
too much

and never enough.

One Day – Tori Louise (she/her)

It is such a shame
That such
A Killer Outfit

Could be ruined
By an absence
Of Consent
Or the memory of it

Unfortunate
That this
Beautiful Body
Should be
Tormented
By unwelcome hands

Once

Again

The morning after
As I surveyed the damage
And quietly reminded myself The
Bruises would fade
In a few days

Leaving a fresh canvas
To be painted
with the fruits of my joys That I
choose
For myself

The inevitable
Fall
With wheels strapped to my feet

Clumsily
Bumping into tables
As in my excitement

I have the luxury
Of moving coordination
To the bottom of my priorities

And I knew that one day
I would soon forget
Among all the other bruises
The ones which I did not choose

I pulled off
The fishnet stockings
And I was proud of how far
I'd dragged my mind
From thinking

The circumstances
Would have been different
If my legs were covered

I did not throw them away Even
though
I desperately wanted to
Even though
There were gaping holes
where none had been before

What do holes matter anyway

In fishnets
I knew
As I Shoved
Them deep
In the bottom of my drawer That
one day
I would wear them
Again

The holes would get bigger And
new ones would form From roller
skating
And Dancing
And Welcome Hands

And I knew that one day
I wouldn't care to remember Which
holes formed first

And though I knew
For a time
I would hate
That I lived in this body

That I would want to stuff myself
In the bottom corner of a drawer
Or Plunge into the void

I knew that one day
That if I waited
With time I would again
slip back
Into my body
With as much comfort
as I do my favorite blue velvet dress
And I knew that one day would
be able
To look myself in the eye And
forget
That I ever wanted to leave

And I knew that one day
I would again don
That killer outfit
And take pleasure
In the beauty of my body
Without fear

I knew that one day
I wouldn't even spare
A moment's thought to
unwelcome hands

Imaginary – Tori Louise (she/her)

I wanted
to be a model
when I was
7 years old
my older sister did
I wanted
to be everything
my sister was

Watching hours of
America's
Next Top Model

Femininity dissected
into bite size portions

Wrapped
in single use plastic

Self-image
placed on shelves
Sold
Freedom of choice
Marketable

The FDA recommends a 2000 calorie diet
Perfectly balanced
Youth, purity, innocence
Sex, depravity, violence

I stared in the mirror
And practiced for the one thing
I was sure I could be

I analyzed the instincts in my body
The shapes it naturally filled

And I corrected
A breath in
Head slightly tilted

Legs quietly tensed
Hands gracefully relaxed
Soften your smile
Pour out the thoughts so they don't wrinkle your face

A body that was a template for desire
Eyes that had been emptied to make room for the reflection of the world Tunnels to
a mind that was hollow
Porcelain skin ready to be filled
With your dreams
Your fantasy
Your reality
Your children

A child
Welcomes a new imaginary friend
Opens the door into her mind and body and beckons them inside
Someone to witness
How good I am at being good
See how well I prepare myself for my role
See how I collect laughs and arrange them on my closet shelves
Ready to be tried on at a sensible time
See how I add new movements to this dance
A repertoire of the best
Beautiful women
I have seen
I study them
As you consume me
And I hope that my performance will be good enough that you stay after the curtain falls

Object(ive) – Tori Louise (she/her)

The more I learn the less control I feel
The more angry I am
So much of reality is dictated by forces beyond our control
It has been going on for so long that we don't even realize it's happening.

People run from the truth because it is painful
It is irreconcilable with existence in natural reality
I cannot separate myself from god, from men, from white supremacy.
We are all imprisoned by reality
One that has been built by our ancestors
I am expected to smile as I form the bricks to lay on the graves of future generations.

We're supposed to ignore it
A lifetime of anger and discomfort and isolation
No one would choose to feel that by themselves
It is better to go on living separate lives
Happily isolated from truth.

My existence is for the consumption of others
I have been curated by society to perform my role
That of creator
A vessel for future generations
The fulfillment of desire

They don't care
How I fulfill my duty
Only that I do
Our labor and our freedom was contested in the past
And so they changed it
Subtly, telling us that we are now equals
Bequeathing us with freedom of choice
They could no longer exploit us en masse
In our homes, for our labor, our bodies, our lives
So they allowed us to join the workforce
Supplementing for the loss
They traded outright violence for the illusion of choice
Told us we had autonomy over our bodies and our lives
But whatever we choose we are exploited

If we are to conform, then we are oppressed
If we are to be liberated, then we are consumed
We do the selling for them
And call it self love
While we pretend that our existence is not a commodity
To be placed on a shelf

I cannot be ugly, for then I must hate myself, and I will be punished for my defects.
I cannot love my beauty without loving the chains of my captors.
Beauty. Goodness. Whiteness. Purity. Truth. Objectivity.
None exist without us there to give them quality.

And here I am
Possessing qualities that have been assigned to me without my conscious knowledge or consent
Defined by that which does not exist
Forced by that unreality to live in a reality which I did not choose
But that which is very real
And if only
We all collectively decided
To cast aside
That which does not exist
To refuse to conform to unreality
To refuse to be prisoners
We would be free
The prison exists in our minds

Its hold on reality is only as strong as those of us who uphold it

Such a simple thing
To exist in reality
And yet
So impossible

the hidden weapon – Lindsay Valentin (she/they)

just in case you thought I wasn't safe coming home to
just in case you thought it unnatural that you love me,
that I love you
just in case of that
I learned to know how to sleep alone at night
not to the left or right
but in the center of an empty bed
just in case you couldn't handle female to female passion
couldn't manage the raw emotion
the judgement
the rough ocean of society
just in case of that
I learned to be independent
learned to hide my heart like a weapon
just in case
just in case you decided you could be outed
just in case it was worth more than your reputation
your obligation
your conformity
just in case of that
I take my weapon from its place of hiding
and place it on the table

we made us – Lindsay Valentin (she/they)

we made us in a way
so they could not break us
so they could not burn us
could not extract us by our roots
so they could not take us

like rainbows
we were born to glow and celebrate
unable to be ripped up
torn out, relegated

we made us
so they could not fade us
so they could not forsake us, remake us,
erase us or incarcerate us

we made us so our blood runs like rivers
so our souls burn like fire
so we've got lambda iron in our livers

we made us
as they tried to degrade us
they did not know
that we were our own creators

the pulp of oneself – Lindsay Valentin (she/they)

and so I fell under the giant yucca
smoky mesquite
my heart space clouded in vapors
rough to feel clearly
through to the origins
after a ten hour soul conversation
where she broke open like
sacred fruit
thrown from its tree
overripe, so sweet
past a kind of point

she says she wants to feel me
but she doesn't believe god
intended us to be this way
together

ripe fruit mixed where lay together
seeds, nectary strands, pink flesh
our souls mixed up in the mesquite

tomorrow she'll disappear as vapor
after our breath syncing together
because she says
the bible deems it unnatural
although she reaches for me
as I look toward the sky
under the spiritual agave

I say I've given it up to you
I've looked in me and know what love is

but some darkness is buried so deep
I love you she says
as she picks up the pulp of herself
and hurls it
into the weeds

Yesterday's sacrarium – Theresa K. Jakobsen (they/them)

Acrylic paint on canvas
Size: 50x70

***Furor Uterinus* – Sarah Blakely** (she/her)

Oh, the fury.

The fury of the womb,
and what it means to carry one inside of you.
The fury of femaleness,
cold biological names for what I am,
for the anger I hold,
woven into my mitochondrial DNA,
anger towards men who have never been
and will never be
a woman.

Oh, the madness.

The madness of menstruation,
that monthly reminder that pain is a part of life.
The blood and blame,
staining names and hands red,
guilty of imagined crimes,
conjuring up spectral evidence,
imagining murder and sin and devil worship,
but why would I worship
a man?

Ask Me What I Like – Sarah Blakely (she/her)

When a man asks me
what I like in bed,
I tend to tell him
what he wants to hear.

That I am dirty,
filthy from being
repeatedly shoved into the ground
face-first.

I like it rough,
like the jagged edges
of shattered glass,
because I am broken.

I want to feel his machismo,
beating into my body
like the gavel that decided
I am not worthy of justice.

Like the hammer and nail
that boarded up my heart,
trapping me inside my own body,
an animal with no way out.

When a man asks me
what I really like,
I will tell him honestly.
I'm not sure.

I like the feeling
of lips meeting,
introducing themselves sweetly
like the sun gently rising in the morning.

I like tender touching,
carefully caressing,
playfully pawing,
when fingers feel like feathers on my skin.

I like palms pressed together
perceiving the pulsing,
the pleasure and excitement
of studying your rhythmic love.

I like knowing
my body is safe,
but I rarely find a man
who is shield instead of spear.

The Self-Proclaimed Nice Guy – Sarah Blakely (she/her)

He's saying I'm being a bitch
but what did I do to deserve this?
Is it because I said "no"?
He's got to learn how to let go.

He calls himself a nice guy
as he complains and wonders why
none of the girls want to talk to him
while he's quietly stalking them.

He says to let him explain,
but I don't want to entertain
his bad behavior and sad excuses,
why can't he just accept when a woman refuses?

Suddenly I'm afraid for my life
as he approaches my house with a knife,
and it will be my fault for not knowing self-defense.
How the hell does that make any sense?

It's a crime in itself how often we women
are threatened to be turned into shades of crimson,
streaks on the sidewalk, police walk over this violence
because it's not a crime scene until someone's lying lifeless.

Abortion Should Not Be A Synonym For Danger – Sarah Blakely (she/her)

When an ultrasound reveals small signs of unborn life,
why is my full-grown body
suddenly secondary?

Why am I an outlaw, a refugee,
my right to choose—
unconstitutional?

Why am I reminded of blood,
gushing crimson, and pain,
the result of a back alley operation?

Why are old white men in stuffy suits
still in control of my body,
restricting my reproductive rights?

Why do they care so much
if there's a heartbeat in my uterus,
are they forgetting about the one beating in my chest?

Why does it feel like being
raped, being unsafe,
all because my womanhood is a fucking debate?

Girls Gone Feral – Sarah Blakely (she/her)

Girls gone feral
after domestication
by men who want a
woman clean-shaven,
to give up her body
as a humble donation.

Girls gone feral
demand an amputation
from men who want a
pretty conversation
to last longer than their
sexual duration.

Girls gone feral
want domination
of men who want a
woman's sensation,
dripping and needy,
feels like holy salvation.

Girls gone feral
cause agitation
in men who want a
woman's admiration,
craving that helpless
look of adoration.

Girls gone feral
learn flirtation
with men who want a
physical confrontation,
turning aggression
into an excavation.

Girls gone feral
have a reputation
towards men who want a
woman's devastation,
but these women
have no obligation.

Girls gone feral
evoke temptation
in men who want a
kingly coronation
while developing a dark
rape culture fixation.

hallowed winter – Lilith Kerr (she/they)

up north, the ice never thaws and the sky grows bloodless and waxen.
here, november is the month of creeping grief;
mercuric entropy with a mouthful of teeth.
4 pm draws a curtain across the city like a mortuary blanket.
        sorrow without a name, without form or body or any trace of heat.
[i never know what to do with myself when the night falls so quickly].

Talk me down – Lilith Kerr (she/they)

I have this recurring dream; The kind of dream that settles in the marrow of your bones, etches itself into the corners of your mind. Here, It's always the verge of nightfall and it's always winter. Winter, as in fuse skin to muscle, freeze your tongue to the roof of your mouth.
My hands press into the gunmetal of the railing—feel it bite like a wild animal into flesh (cold so sharp it feels like burning). I clamber, feet over hands over heart onto the far side of the barrier.
Every night, the story changes, just a little. Barely perceptible, it shifts a touch to the right, moves things around. But in every version, the water remains—thrashing and hungry; its waves open like a maw.
I pull thickets of January air into my lungs like the action alone could carve an epitaph into the gore of my side. I reach forward. I step into empty space.

And my stomach lunges out of my body.

Because I'm not falling, but instead held aloft over the cratering of air below me. Hand on my wrist, hand on my waist, hand on my arm, hand on my hand. And I'm on solid ground and someone is brushing the tangle of hair back from my sweat-soaked face. And I'm catharsis like an unbecoming, sitting on the pavement and unraveling, falling into rivulets. Big, heavy, racking sobs that hollow themselves into the dark of my abdomen.
And for once, I'm not the one doing the saving. I allow myself to be the damsel in distress; to have them bundle me in their arms and wrap all my trembling up into a heavy coat. To let them hold me gently, with no ulterior motives.
Because the thing is,

I've never wanted to be loved so much as saved—
desired so much as talked
down from a steep height.

unconditional – Lilith Kerr (she/they)

call me wanted.
call me yours,
call me loved without making me sit up and beg for scraps;
without bisecting the pulp of my chest and eating my heart bloody.
call me worthy even when my mind tethers itself to death and breaks bread with the reaper.
show me i can be loved fully-clothed—take me home without undressing me,
without pressing
my body
against a wall and
your hands
between my thighs.
could you love me simply—without any strings attached?

Unapologetically Woman – Brooke Gerbers (she/they)

I don't hate being a woman but
Sometimes my skin stretches in ways I did not give it permission to
Sometimes my eyes read more invitation than warning
And the curve of my spine resembles my mother's too closely

Sometimes my hips feel like unwanted house guests inside of men's cargo pants
And my hands keep a running tally of all the times they've been considered too small
My heart will cave the first time the right person uses the word "pretty"
And I've learned to store teardrops safely in their tear ducts
Because boys don't cry
But neither do tough girls
And I've pretended to be both

I skip like a broken record every time I say that soft and weak are not synonymous

I don't hate being a woman but
It's taken 7 years to learn that the title can stand on its own
Without needing the prefix—victim
Or the suffix—survivor

I am human just as much as I am woman
I am holy just as much as I am whole

Take Me out of My Skin – Brooke Gerbers (she/they)

I have been carving your name out of my skin
With broken tequila bottles for the better part of 7 years
I have attempted to make space between my thighs for gentle hands
And space behind my ribcage for gentle hearts
I have failed at both more times than the words "don't cry"
Have danced through the shadows of my thoughts in your voice

I have talked about it a lot in therapy

I have used anger as a morning affirmation
As an addiction
As a religion
And my therapist says that the most important tools serve many purposes
That it is okay to use and reuse them as many times as I need

I hold this toolbelt in my throat

But sometimes it's in the space between dusk and dawn
And sometimes it lives in the corner of half-smiles
And sometimes it sits with me in the shower
when I can't seem to peel myself off the floor of it

It's been 7 years since I've gone into the bar on the corner of St. Joe Center Rd. and Clinton
6 and a half since you asked if I wanted you to bus my tables—
Your sorry attempt to clean up the mess you'd made
And 4 since I left the city you threw a black veil over and named Death

I am not angry anymore

Sometimes I wake up at 3 am and feel like my bones are lying right next to yours—again
But I'm better at holding myself
sometimes I see you in every white middle-aged man's face at the grocery store
but I'm better at focusing on my reflection on the doors in the frozen aisle instead
Sometimes it hurts too much to think about
Other times it pours out over coffee with a stranger

And my therapist says that there is no right way to heal
But that I am doing just that

Among the Unlikeable Parts – Brooke Gerbers (she/they)

I've studied my anatomy in the mirror at every angle—
Twice.
First with skepticism
Then with something just shy of acceptance.
This body has become an array of bright colors
But I've only ever known how to read it in braille,
And this foreign language is not something I am well versed in.
I've attempted to dog-ear pieces of skin into waistlines—
A mind game I like to play
To convince myself that these are the parts worth coming back to and rereading.
They have always been the parts that receive the most attention after all.
They say it takes 66 days for a behavior to become automatic
But I would argue that science is no match for determination.
I mastered the art of making this body a graveyard in seconds,
Does anyone know how long it takes to break a habit?
Or least how to break a tombstone?

Before You Say Yes – Brooke Gerbers (she/they)

I've learned to present this body as an apology letter
I'm sorry, no, don't put your hands there
I'm sorry, yes, there are still places inside these bones even I won't visit

The truth is I wish I had less explaining to do
I'm sorry, yes, I still sleep with the lights on
I'm sorry, no, there is not an inch of smooth skin left for your tongue to trace

I could tell you about how many times I've lost myself in the breaking of my spine
But I couldn't tell you where to come find me in the middle of a nightmare
I'm sorry, no, I'll never be able to have a glass of wine with you
I'm sorry, yes, I think I'll always be searching for the next place that feels like home

I can't guarantee that you'll be able to find a seat comfortable enough to sit in—
To stay in
I'm sorry, yes, there are still some pieces I am trying to glue back together
I'm sorry, no, I will never be a thing that is completely habitable

I have learned that it is impossible to apologize for a body that no longer belongs to me
But damnit, I'll try,
I'll try

Good woman – Brooke Gerbers (she/they)

I have never been a good woman

And maybe my mother is to blame
For putting me in baseball
Instead of dance
So that my fingernails
Were always covered in dirt
Instead of sparkly nail polish

Or maybe my father is to blame
Because in his household
Being woman meant
Being punching bag
But ever since I was young
I wanted to be the one boxing
Hands taped
Ready for a damn good fight
But he said:

That's not how good women behave

I have never behaved like a good woman
I walk into a room
All five foot six of me
With the voice of a giant
And a demand to be heard

I turn Venus Fly Trap
When I feel threatened
And my guilty pleasure
Is feasting on my prey

I refuse to sit
In the corner of the room
Invisible
Polite
Poised

And watch as the other good women
Get picked off
By the "good men"
After they've been fed too many

Instead I turn tornado
And pick off the good men
While I simultaneously turn shelter
To save the good women
From the storm

I am not delicate
I am not eye-candy
And I am not someone to be tampered with

I have never been a good woman

But
I am still a woman

And just once
I want to be able to say
I am a woman
Without it sounding like an
Amusing joke
Or
An invitation
Or
A death sentence
Just once
I want to be able to say
I am a woman
And watch as they bow down
One by one
Because just once
I want to be able to say
I am a woman
So fiercely
That the weight of those words
Brings them to their
Knees

Bonfire night. - Tara Dudhill (she/her)

I am in the dark in love
with the idea of you
                                        and I
and what we might have been.

Burning bright, brilliant
with the glow of being seen.

Or dimmer, love, with these other eyes
on the sky, our hands could clasp,
and melt into night. A good time,
                                                            at least,
with you, who I would never ask for a long time.

But instead, worlds away, while I dream of words,
                                                                        your hand reaches out
                                                                                        and clasps into his
and he pulls you inside his winter coat
                                        and I grasp at straws
and the fire paints you golden
                          and I breathe in your smoke

and it drifts   from me,   a shadow   in   the   dusk.

Before – Julie Elefante (she/her)

We're looking at the lineup,
at outcasts, undesirables, criminals,
our "Before" photos;
everyone hates their Before,
disowns them,
"That isn't Me."
Now we are sleeker, slimmer,
lean
lean in so many things.
I look at my Before, see
eyes dark and lonely,
defiant,
carrying weight beyond her frame,
diabetic, hypertensive,
her very heart damaged,
from unabled to disabled.
Eyes so deep,
I dive in
to her strength, her drive—
Fighter. She had my back
when others diminished me to ugly;
she saw worth, hope, a life worth saving,
worth living—
I want her, need her,
love her every ounce;
she is me,
Before, Now, and All Ways.

Language – Julie Elefante (she/her)

Ano ampangalan mo?
What is your name?
Ako ay sig Julie.
My name is Julie.
Ako ay eeyong anak.
I am your daughter.
Paanosasabhim.
Teach me your language so I can tell you…
I sit at your table
Learning the words
Rehearsing the sounds
Chasing you down
Paanosasabhim salt…pepper…table…chair.
I want to learn words that you'll hear
That your ears are open to
Paanosasabhim car…glass…water…flower.
What were the words you grew up hearing
Before you came here?
Paanosasabhim thank you…
you always cared for me
Always sacrificed for me
And I'm writing as many words as I can phonetically
So I can remember
So I don't forget to tell you
Because language is the barrier
That breaks the mother-daughter bond
Because you have a wealth of stories to share
And I want to inherit your history
My history
Because you brought me over
on the boat of the
bowed back of your body
while I was still a piece of fiction
waiting to come true
ako ay eeyung anak
ekow an nanayko

we are not breaking bonds
but building them
brick by brick
upwards
onwards
moving on
And it's not enough to say
Ito ay asin
Ito ay pamenta
Ito ay le mesa
Ito ay silya
Inefficient when I say
Eeyuna oto
Eeyuna vaso
Eeyuna bulaclac
Eeyuna tubig
The words don't flow fast enough
And I stutter and trip
Over the wrinkles around your eyes
With time
You teach me the phrase I've been waiting for
Mahal kita
Mahal namahal kita.

Empty, Full – Julie Elefante (she/her)

Some don't know what to say to those grieving.
Some try to say everything.
That was my boss—a curated collection of "grief is" statements,
but I've been salvaging through aftermaths for my own,
banking them for the perfect comeback.

A Teams meeting message: "Hello, how are you?"
Do I answer honest or false?

Hello, this is empty.
Hello, this is full.

The first grief is simple:
it's dry heaves and tears.
The next griefs try to be everything.

Grief is a speck, precise and sharp.
Grief is a miniscule all.
Grief is a universe, multitudes, unknowable.

I learned:
My mother traced the constellations of illness inside her belly,
a universe of unsung myths dancing and battling around her breaths,
she named them after ancient regrets,

the keening onomatopoeia of the word "weep,"

she'd been so lonely since my dad died
just three years past;
she'd forgotten how much she loved him.
No matter how it happens,
the heart breaks most when you stop taking someone for granted,
when the vacuum of their absence forever steals a crucial breath away.

So now my brothers and I are orphans

hello, this is empty, hello this is full:

Grief is the house and everything in it,
all the hoarded things and the vast emptiness they contain.

My mom wasn't violent,
but a fist in life
and remained clenched as she lay dying;
we always fought
but never said sorry—
Mom was the knife, the stab,
Grief is the cut, the blood, the scab.

It's the pain in my chest and the echoes of beats that reverberate in it,
the ancient regrets passed down like a birthright,

Grief is an egg
a membrane, a shell
something formless inside trying to gather itself into sentience,
to break free.
To weep. To speak.
Grief is all the words you know,
all the chances you missed to say them,
my heart aching, hatching
into my body,
birthing the world as it's never been before.

Hello, this is empty.
Hello, this is full.

Grief is losing.
Empty
Grief is loving.
Full.
Grief is living.

Mother Redefined – Julie Elefante (she/her)

Growing up, I loved the idea that my Dad was a hero...
I would bother my father
and ask him what it was like in Vietnam,
and he'd say, "We would build a bridge in a day,
and the next it would be blown away,"
before stopping, slipping
into the parched, yellow silence of his memories,
his lips pursed to keep the war far and away from his family...
But while he fought like a brave man
against the Vietcong, on the home front was my mother,
trying to be strong,
on tour of the world towing one son, two sons,
three sons, four sons from port to base to port to base
keeping on her brave face from place to place—
you'll be in Hawaii, you'll go to Oakland,
down to Port Hueneme, to Gulfport, Mississippi
to Yokuska, then to Iwakuni
back to Hueneme,
living your life in circles, racing after your tail,
thinking what will you do if something happens to him and he's gone ...
where do you go from here?
are you following or being chased by fear?

My mother's accent painted auditory arrows at herself ,
pointing her out as an Asian foreigner,
not necessarily Filipino, because they weren't common enough
to be known—labeled—she was all alone with her children–
a bunch of Chinese, or Japanese,
or some other "yellow-skinned disease,"
she, with her short, small stature and black, long hair
hidden in a proper bun,
feet bound-clad in stockings and modest pumps.
I wonder now if she was ever made to feel ashamed,
ever felt the same as I did in my grade school classes–
back then, she was a just controlling mother
who would smother me with what she wanted me to be—

a woman like she was who could cook and care for her family
before herself, because her family is her self,
the ultimate incarnation of who she is:
mother, wife, birth, life, and she tried to make me be like her,
everything I was seeing a direct product of her point of view,
no matter how old-fashioned and skewed it was,
but it wasn't all oppression, it was partly tradition she was passing down
like how to cook the rice with our daily meals,
habit-forming grains seeding our brains with ideas of her sacrifice.

I try now to cling to the words of the songs
my mother would sing in the kitchen
while she cooked and cleaned,
trying to teach an unwilling daughter
in her duty as a housewife and mother,
but later, the words gave way to hums
as if the words had been forgotten;
I wish my ears had tuned in to the stories
she told—her voice would carry the melodies
of present memories into my head for storage.

When the battle came down to the fear of being kept from my culture,
I realized she had ingrained a sense of Filipino being in me,
helped me know that, like she,
I am a hyphenated woman with an identity crisis,
taught me to say, "you cannot dash my spirits
it's a fine line between who I am, want to be, and try to be,
but there's a point to my existence, and that is to define me."

I draw reference from her bravery,
how she kept breathing through insecurity—
from the life she could have had,
but gave up to make five lives out of one
in the most heroic way she knew how.

Touch Me – Mo McMasters (they/them)

Stone Heart – Korbyn McKale (she/her)

The night of my uncle's funeral I went home alone.
My empty house swallowed me, hungry for emotion,
unsatisfied with me. I laid in bed, stared dryly
at the funeral program inside my trash can.

Indifference is somehow more painful than sadness.
Nothing releases pressure from a bursting heart like tears,
yet stone was the only thing in my chest.
His kids couldn't even remember the last time they saw him.

I didn't miss him, I didn't even love him. I thought
my father didn't either, but I watched him fight
tears in God's house. After years of begging him to man up,
to straighten out, maybe overdosing was his way of freeing everyone.

/

A friend invited me to his house so I wouldn't have to be
alone. To be held and feel human sounded better
than solitude, but his touch knew nothing of humanity.
It only understood vulnerability. He didn't listen
when I told him I wanted his shoulder, not his hands.

There is something in humans that tricks them into believing
they know better than other people, better than a girl, especially.
He had wanted to help, to give me something to feel, but the heavy
numbness of the day spread into my every cell. My resistance pinned
by the weight. Stone limbs, stone voice, stone cognition.

My body was not my own and yet, somehow, I had given it
to him. It doesn't seem like a crime if no one puts up a fight.
My stone heart lay still with me in bed,
marked the second grave of the day.

Garden/Body/Prison – Korbyn McKale (she/her)

If she had the choice
she would plant lavender
seeds in her veins, wait
for joy to sprout from her eyes,

but she does not get to decide
what grows in her garden anymore.
Her blood waters the soil, her teeth plow
hundreds of rows every spring.

She is the only one who tends the fruits
of the garden that keep her alive—
the only one that fights with blunt force
and bare skin the creatures that try to ravage it.

Even after a beast tore through, uprooted
every perfect petal, she alone bloodied
her hands resowing, rebuilding, breaking
her back to reclaim her sacred space

and still this garden is no longer her own.
If she could, she would swallow indigo and lilac,
hold them in her throat, savor the gentle brush of petal, but
every woman knows her body is not a place deemed for flowers.
She wonders if it ever was.

After I Forgot to Check Under the Bed,
I Found We Are All Monsters – Korbyn McKale (she/her)

I am afraid of the dark now.
Not for monsters, but for men. Men
that use the dark. When I imagine
him, he is always in his cell. I wonder
if he is afraid of the dark now, too.
Afraid of the men inside it.
Part of me hopes he is.
But every time I think of him lying
in the night, he is not cowering,
not kneeling, not crying.
In the dark in my mind
he is always smiling.

Trapped Butterfly – K.G. Munro (she/her)

Reflection in the same window,
Waiting for the night to come,
So that the moonlight can hide her shadow,
As she runs,
Raven dress and silky long hair,
Her skin is like starlight,
A black butterfly is tattooed behind her left ear; a mark of imprisonment,
She grabs her cotton cloak before running to the stone stairs,
Each tap reverberates across palace walls,
Travelling like a ghost across these halls,
Her handlers are at a conference tonight,
This is her shot at freedom as she takes different passageways,
For years they have brainwashed and tortured her,
She finally was able to free her mind when she saw the moonlight,
The first time, many days ago,
Now she is running to get back her life,
The scent of pine fills her nose with fresh air,
Imprisoning warmth no longer restraining her,
As she finally makes it outside,
Holding her cloak closer to her body,
She continues to run,
Past the dark green trees and branches,
Her feet burn as the twigs snap beneath her feet,
The forest seems to be endless,
Moonlight glows brightly over her,
Time melts into nothingness,
Until she finds an opening,
Loud voices start echoing,
She gives it everything,
As she practically dives out of the woods,
And lands onto the cold road,
The woods behind her finally disappear,
Flying away the black butterfly departs from her skin,
As she looks up to see nothing there,
Just the golden sun rising,
For the first time in years.

Leslie and Rebecca – Moriah Katz (she/her)

She came quicker than I thought she would. Steps too confident for someone her age—someone our age—which is sixty-three but would suffice to say *old.* I thought her feet were going to bust through the steps when she stomped onto the porch. I opened the door before she could knock.

"Buenas dee-yas!"

She scoffed. "Buen-os. I can see you haven't been practicing."

She hugged me despite my flub. She was always like that. Generous. I fended off what I could of her generosity with pats to her back. I blushed and blamed it on my Spanish. "I haven't. No one to practice with these days."

Her smirk slipped as I locked the door. She noticed my tremoring hands and the shuffle that interrupted my gait. I'd changed a lot since the accident.

"I was wondering how you'd been. I tried to call but—"

"I got the flowers you sent to the hospital. Those were more than enough. Thank you."

"So, no more fútbol?"

I shrugged, "The doctors tell me to be hopeful."

"Ah, you got a young one, didn't you?"

"How'd you know?"

"Mine are always old and good at reminding me I'm gone over the hill."

I laughed. It felt so good I did it again, just for kicks. Becca put her hand on my shoulder and kept it there. My cheeks ran hot. She held my gaze and my cheeks ran hotter. She opened her mouth and I leaned in, expecting something I was scared to admit.

"Can you take my coat?"

I took a step back. She shrugged out of her flimsy windbreaker and held it above the carpet. Beads of rain dripped down the fabric and flattened themselves into tiny puddles on the floor. I hung it on an empty coat rack screwed into a naked wall. Milk crates, stuffed to the brim with my life, took up every other available wall space. I gestured to a chair in front of the tv. "I've only got one chair. Please, take it."

She took a few steps toward it, then turned on her heel, "Actually, do you mind if I take a bath? I kind of got soaked through."

I stumbled toward the bathroom.

"I remember where it is."

"Ok, there's towels in the—"

"I remember that, too."

I left her to flounce across the islands of memory that blocked the walkway to the bathroom. The pile of abandoned soccer jerseys. The tupperware my ex-husband bought me when he heard about the accident. Manila folders stuffed with every piece of mail I've received since I came home from the hospital.

She was a picture of everything I should have been. Strong legs resisting all signs of varicose. A full set of perfect teeth. When she disappeared around the corner, I thought about the lines she had, how hers were in happier places. Around the corners of the eyes and mouth. I touched my own face. A maze of worry lines criss-crossing my forehead, a leathery cheek losing itself to the sagging disappointment under my chin. It is unfair what life will take from you.

I dip a bag of hibiscus in a mug of hot water. A commercial for life insurance drones on in the background. *Just enough to cover our funeral costs, medical bills, credit cards.* What a strange order, I think. I remind myself to buy life insurance. There is a steady stream of advertisements that follow: antidepressants, arthritis medication, and Pepto Bismol. My thoughts float on their surface like tea lights. One winks at me from down river and whispers my name. It is so hard to hear from all the way around the bend. On the counter, the hibiscus has bled fully into the mug.

"Leslie. LES-LIE!"

I struggle down the hall to the bathroom door. My life gets in the way. I stumble. I clutch at the doorknob to avoid falling. I knock twice. Becca calls out, her voice muffled on the other side of the door. I knock again. The same tangle of sound comes to me, more song than word. I swallow the thought of Rebecca alone, the clawfoot tub cradling her naked body. I turn the knob and collapse onto the damp floor.

"I said," she says, up to her neck in water, her knees a pair of mountains interrupting a sea of bubbles, "come in."

"I didn't hear you."

"Obviously."

The faucet dashes and dots through our silence. I swallow again.

"What did you want?"

"Well, you know, I am an old woman. And getting out of this tub is proving harder than I remember it being. And there's no goddamned rail here. I'm surprised you didn't have one installed after. Well, you know."

"After I almost died getting out of the tub?" Her knees sink a little deeper beneath the water. Seconds pass before I realize she is embarrassed. I sigh, "Here."

I hold out my hand to help her stand. I am careful not to stare at her sagging breasts, the loose and stretch-marked skin of her tummy. I pass her a towel and ignore the tissue-paper softness of her shoulder as my thumb brushes against it. I tell myself it is an accident. She grabs a comb from the vanity and holds it out to me imperiously.

"I'm getting deja vu."

She ignores me and parts her long, silver hair into two sections. The last time she'd been here like this, I'd caught the first few of her hairs to go gray in the sea of black. I'd teased her about getting old then. That was thirty years ago.

I inched toward the tub, and she pretended not to notice. So much was the same about her. That same terra cotta skin, that chocolate colored birthmark still melting down her neck like ice cream forgotten in the sun. I ran my index over it, then followed a bead of sweat down her shoulder and into the bath water. She sighed. My stomach became a fist. She spoke first, "I wasn't sure I wanted this."

"I was. You wanted it last time."

"That was a long time ago."

I paused the comb halfway through her hair. "True. But we have less to lose now."

"Really?" she said, twisting her head to face me. The comb clattered too loud against the tile floor. She ignored it and pressed her forehead to the flat space over my heart. My arms wrapped themselves around her shoulders. My hands shook less than normal. "I'd think we'd have more, no?" she whispered into my shirt.
"Well," I thought back to the first and only time we'd done this. The room felt smaller then. Everything was longing drawn taught in the steam. There was the seamlessness of our bodies as we searched for each other's centers. Making love had been painfully delicious. "We don't have any husbands to miss us, children to want us, parents to judge us."

"Mmm. But friends?"

Her words left a question-mark shaped cloud of condensation under my collar. I thought back to the day I fell. I hated that I couldn't forget it. I'd taken off the gray plastic box that I usually hung around my neck from a cheap lanyard. I put it on the sink counter. It was waterproof, like the commercial had promised, but I needed a moment of my day without it. Just one moment not yoked to calamity.

I sunk into my bath and closed my eyes. The red lettering from the commercial glowed behind my eyelids. *When You FALL and Cannot Get Up, an ACCIDENT can turn into a TRAGEDY.* What obnoxious capitalization. The rats scuttled in the attic. I wondered about their lives until my body pruned. I rose out of the tub, reached for my towel, and then—

My feet slid across the bone-white tiles. I split my head on the lip of the sink still wet with Listerine from my morning routine. I heard the bone crack. The walls stretched into impossibly high ceilings. The steam rolled off my tangled, useless legs. Pain bloomed in my temple. I bled and bled and bled. The world grew quiet. I couldn't hear the rats. I began to miss them. I reached for the ugly plastic box, the bright red button at its center. My arms were so heavy, and my head was splitting open wide along some invisible seam. The last thought I had as my fingers closed around that ugly little box was, *I always knew I'd die alone.* "Leslie. Leslie, you're crying."

"We can..." the fist in my stomach tightens harder. "We can let them figure out what they want to figure out. That's all."

Rebecca bent to the floor then, surprisingly spry for her age, our age of sixty-three. I hated her for it. Why had I been the one to get hurt? I'd been stronger, faster, smarter about everything. I'd accomplished more, followed all the rules, and still—

"Look at me."

And so I did. I'd intended to stay angry, to keep that first clenched tight in my middle. But it relaxed like a petal in bloom, and I luxuriated in the soft folds of skin that rested against one another on her body. I traced the curve of her, beginning at her birthmark, down the crooked line of her arms, past the scarred and bruised knees. I rested my thumb against a single varicose vein spider webbing across her thigh. She cupped my chin, and I dragged my eyes across the paunch of skin above her pubis, over the flat breasts that narrowed into brown nipples pointing toward the floor. She opened her mouth and I drew her into me like breath. She was warm and soft and thinner than paper. She ran her tongue over my lips, then my teeth. She tasted the valleys I hadn't bothered to fill with partials, the places where bone had fallen out since we'd last held each other in this bathroom.

"Huh," she said, smiling. "That's new."

I laughed, winded by everything that had changed since then.

Breathe – Dawn Wing (she/her)

MY land – Ananiah J (she/her)

My land is barren/
but not because rain doesn't grace it/
it receives just enough/
fields surrounding mine grow/
with fruits and vegetables/
I watch as women toil all day/
with their dresses bunched around their knees/
under the heat of the burning sun/
planting, ploughing, watering from dawn to dusk.
But my land is barren/
I don't like being asked why it doesn't grow/
I never ask why you do grow in yours/
and when those without a field ask so/
I say, "why, you have no field at all".
People barging into my house with sacks of seed/
"I've got enough," I say shutting my door on them/
"I've got enough"/
and I'm happy/
happy I get to see other fields growing so green and bright/
happy in my barren, barren land/
and I know that I do not want to be a farmer/
ever.

I'm sorry I ruined your wedding – Ananiah J (she/her)

I fall right through the glass ceiling
Hanging by the chandelier, I weigh it down
Pricks of glass stab into my poor heart
And I bleed above everyone seated
Two girls dressed in white watch as red spills onto them
Inch by inch, it wrecks their satin
I catch a glimpse of you
Horror on your face, but you stay fixed
Your hand in another's, as you watch
Like everyone else does
As my heart smashes right through the lacy white of the cake
Now I can say proudly that I've given you my all
To me, this death is heavenly (even heroic maybe)
With the single breath left in my cloudy, black lungs
I choke out the only words I wish you'd sew straight into my dainty, red heart.

Hold her – Ananiah J (she/her)

I find the wooden box
Hidden beneath the floorboards
Pictures of you grinning welcome me.
I find one of you pouting in a pink gingham jumper
I remember how you refused to wear anything but that for weeks
I paste it onto the mirror facing the streets of someplace you dreamed of.
My fingers stained pink, for I painted my studio walls
I've bought orchids, tulips, and asters in all the colours that you like
Honeypies, pastries, cookies, and cola lay beneath the sun on the patio.
We could stay up late reading, or maybe we could watch a film
Here is the world you've always wanted, so please come back
Looking inside the four chambers I hunt for a fragment of you.
And sometimes you pass me, like the wind whistling, you call out
I find you at the ice cream store as sprinkles are poured and in the spines of bedtime stories
But it's not the same anymore because I changed and grew (or so they say)
Abandoning you on a flaming ship destined for an island
Now I'm lonely and I wish you'd come home, trust me for once and I promise to hold you in my arms for eternity.

yearned, waited, & prayed – Linda M. Crate (she/her)

"see you're more than a pretty face,"
but i've never seen myself that way;
always knew i was more than this flesh and
these bones—
it is not my fault that you couldn't see
past my outward beauty,
and into the inward beauty of my soul;
you only have yourself to blame
if you're that shallow—
all of my life i have yearned and waited and
prayed for the type of love that exists
in fantasy books where they truly, madly, deeply
love one another and would move the moon
and stars and sun and even the sky for one another
if that was what was required;
but for people like you the garden of my heart
is savage and full of thorns and thistles
and you'll never find my roses—
because if all i am to you is a pretty face
you don't deserve to know the mythology of my bones
or the lyrics of my heart and soul.

miracle and magic exist – Linda M. Crate (she/her)

i tried to pray the gay away,
but that wasn't a prayer
that was ever answered;

guess the universe liked me
as i was—

i never felt safety in sanctuary,
always looked out stained glass
windows praying for answers
that never came;

it turns out their god was not mine—

have never liked confrontations,
but i had to confront everything they taught
me and ask if i believed it, and turns out
there's a lot that i could not agree with;

i believe every person should choose
for themselves and their own life if abortion
is something they want, and i know that
being queer isn't a choice someone makes but
rather how someone is born regardless of
how they're raised, and i don't believe any woman
should have to submit to any man ever—

lost my religion but never my faith, because
i know miracles and magic exist,
but perhaps not in the way they tried to tell us
in churches.

Gusher – Melissa Frederick (she/her)

Life dribbles through my fingers like blood
through a vein, so much quicker and slipperier
than you'd expect fluid to flow through a pinprick,
down a set of concrete stairs, out the sliding glass doors,
branches loose in the air.

Where are my wild children?
These saturated striations will act as a map
to bring you home—back, back, to my denatured body,
unzipped like a polyester evening gown. Holes open
along my ribcage. Holes gape. Holes run.
There is nothing much darker than holes.

But you, my foundlings, are welcome here
under my deflated remains. Hide yourselves well
in my chest cavity, my belly, my thick, drained limbs.
Passersby will treat us like cobblestones.
They ignore what they see as a single mass of death.

But we—you—will crawl out in the dark,
slip away in the fog, find your safe havens
far from here, far from me. My blood will draw out
another map that you will complete. Your next
stopping point awaits. You, the free. You, the brave.

Ceres – Melissa Frederick (she/her)

You measure my craters
like you measure women's curves.
I tell you: the impacts are there
but tamped down by blows that hit next,

another and another and another.
When one fist hits you,
you bruise. When thousands of fists...
ah, that's when the edges vanish,

that's when your icy core
bubbles up to smooth each contusion.
I sparkle, I shine. My frozen heart
greets a vacuum equally harsh

and unrelenting. What I am
is a gravid mother pushing a plow.
bent in threshing,
baby strapped to my back

who will stay bundled
far from the universe and its labors
until it's time to seek relief
in my fat-draped chest.

I tell you: my name
means to feed and grow.

The Bluest Lie – Melissa Frederick (she/her)

On a cloudless night
when war no longer occupies
our conversation. and the fighting
is far away—

physically far, so much so
that we can share a bitter laugh
at the rumbles and crackles
that keep us from sleeping—

that's when I'll tell you
the first blue lie:
how my mother's brother
makes his money.

Maybe we'll stop there.
But if you press me further,
I'll add more to the list:

how the policemen stare
as I work in the garden,
why there is blood smeared
on the porch railing, whether
blood is the cause of a stain
on my sleeve,

the precise times I go to the gas station,
the supermarket, and the bank,
which neighbors I see walking by at noon

and which are still awake
at two in the morning
and what they have just been doing
and what they talk about
when that action is past.

Believe me, in all my days
I have never told so many lies.

Believe me, I despise keeping
truth from you.

your feminism – Marianna Pizzini Mankle (she/her/hers)

There should be no fight
between stay-at-home
and career-holding individuals. our
fight for feminism needs
to hold each in high
regard. the desires of the
heart should not be swayed
by the money in your
pocket book or the partner
on your arm. so please,
dear chosen one,
love your children ferociously
or climb that career
mountain. the organs
of your body do not grant
you permission or deny
you entry: only you can
decide how feminism speaks
for you.

Not Your Villains – Che Flory (they/them)

I wish I could see myself in the hero. I have been trained my whole life to look towards the funny side character or the villain to see anyone who resembles me. It's not like it never happens, but I never assume that the main character is going to feel like me. I don't turn on the TV to find me. Why would I do that? It is inconceivable that I would ever find anything there. I can't even imagine what it would be like to walk into a movie theater and have multiple movies that have a main character that resembles me in them. I am not even that marginalized of an identity. I'm a white, queer person. I've gotten a bit closer with Black queer media, at least the characters aren't constructed from the misprints of the American Dream, but a relatable protagonist is still few and far between. This lack of positive representation has just become a part of my fabric, and I don't really mind it too much. Maybe, I should mind a little more.

Not much can break my heart the way watching a ten-year-old see themself in a villain does. Jafar, Ursula, Scar, Cruella de Vil, Gaston, Captain Hook—all fun characters with some pretty great songs, but a child looking at them and seeing that as their destiny is painful—only being able to perceive a future in which they are there to foil some pretty cishet person's grand plan. The gut-punch—they never succeed; it's always some humiliating failure, sometimes resulting in death. The hero is rarely relatable to marginalized groups, but the villain is. It hurts like hell to see a young person make that correlation. A pre-teen isn't irreparably bad. They aren't there to ruin the world, and our media landscape shouldn't promote this internalization. Children aren't born this bad. Fuck every Calvinist who tells you otherwise. People are good. That is our nature..

I work in character creation and portrayal. Much of the work I create includes heavy subject matter, catered toward an adult audience, but I do have work that is a bit lighter and more inclusive. The diverse characters I get to write are never good people though, at least not the ones who succeed. The majority of the characters I will introduce to the world are leaning toward villainy. At face value, this seems like a decent way to operate in the world, at least a logical one. Adding complex characters to our media landscape is, overall, a good thing. It steers us away from rough outlines of characters—these archetypes can lead to stereotypes, and stereotypes haven't done us much good as a society. In that regard, complex characters are great because people really do act as both the hero and the villain. At the same time, creating mistake-laden diverse characters alongside every other vaguely evil character still feels gross. It is hard to do it right, but I do believe it's possible, even if I haven't fully figured it out.

I am always concerned I am going to create more negative characters for people to find themselves in, and that these characters will not be the prime example of the good of humanity. I don't want to live in a society where the Venn diagram of hedonism and homosexuality is practically a circle, but nearly all hedonistic media, truly it might be every instance I've ever run into, includes a heavy undertone of homoeroticism. Hedonism is an environment I operate within but don't usually partake in; I find it quite difficult to balance art production and hedonism, so I just enjoy the spoils of historical hedonism and some of its modern-day counterparts. Because of my proximity and admiration of those lives, I frequently bring those elements into the things I create. Hedonism mixed with morally grey characters with a very queer cast leads to queer characters repeatedly doing bad things that are going to cater perfectly to an audience that I don't want to be finding solace in these characters.

Queer men, in particular, have a sort of perceived materialism, which adds to this hedonistic ideal projected upon them, but queer people aren't somehow more selfish than the rest of the world. The representation frequently shown is of incredibly selfish characters, which leads to their questionable actions, while portraying sex as a selfish action. Enjoying things, having collections, or just advocating for your humanity are not seen as selfish acts when white cishet people do them, and the same should be true of any other group. The same should be true of sexual preferences. Selfishness isn't an inherently bad thing, but I know we aren't ready for that conversation.

There is a temptation to say that queer people are just normal people, but I don't think I agree with that statement. I don't want to perpetuate the concept of normal because it doesn't exist, and we really should stop pretending it does, but even in terms of a certain population and the expectations of it, so many queer people fall outside of that. Queer people, in a similar vein to other historically oppressed groups, have a specific culture that they have built and now operate within. This is something that falls outside of most populations' norms. There is, and in my opinion always will be, an otherness to the queer community. Though there may be more acceptance, queer people will not ever fully fit in a community other than their own. They can be loved and accepted and appreciated, but there will always be something just different enough about them. In the same way that I will never fully assimilate into my partner's Black family, cishet people will never be able to fully assimilate into the queer culture and vice versa. The inherent otherness combined with the fact that queer people could be anywhere, and you have just failed to recognize them, only adds to the degree of separation between the groups.

The label "queer" tells you that right off the bat. I wanted to make an argument based on the definition of queer, but my search history has assumed my intentions and gave me four explanatory articles on the modern queer experience before finally a Merriam-Webster link to a definition. A shift to an incognito tab did provide me with the information I was looking for, a Google definition box that cited the first definition as "strange or odd". Despite the Internet failing me yet again, I would argue that the point still stands: queerness involves a separation, in our current set-up yet another separate but unequal situation—*Queer people are just like you, they are in your homes and in your schools, and they are just grooming your children while they're at it. Queer people are the normal person's evil sister who has the most malicious of intentions. Are you really sure you want your kids around them?* Don't be fooled, this separation is to protect cishet bodies, but some savvy people might market it as a benefit to the queer community. Equality doesn't look like danger for existing, even in your own separate space. I don't know what that is, but it certainly isn't any better. Queer people are different, but they are beautiful. They shouldn't have to hide away to keep you safe because they aren't a danger.

Maybe the worst part of this all is that I really did internalize it. I still don't feel like I am a good person. I don't believe that I will ever be able to be one. Am I a villain? Logically, probably not. A few people might believe that, but I don't think it is a true statement overall. Without abandon, I make jokes at my own moral expense. I might have some unconventional morals, but I stick to them with an intensity I rarely see elsewhere.

I believe that humanity as a whole is good and beautiful, and I work off of that belief in everything I do. I think that these so-called bad people would probably view people as a little bit more expendable than I ever could. I can rationalize why I must not be in this role they have cast me in. I can actively advocate for a better world for people like me because we are good at our core. I can treat every person I meet with this complex humanity and beauty I believe in. I will never believe it for myself though. I am the failed victim of this mentality, a pretty damn good one, fighting for better and really believing it, but also a person who fell for it all hook, line, and sinker. Why would a good person be like me? Good people aren't passionate and cocky and queer. You are lucky if you can balance two of those with your upstanding moral compass.

To the queer person that only saw themself as the villain and it has seeped into the very fiber of your being, I think you are a pretty stellar person. I'm proud of you. I think you are good. And maybe, you could feel the same for me.

Aces Wild Blackberries – Jillian Calahan (she/her/they)

I was 9 the first time I kissed a boy,
just a quick peck of our lips.
We were too young to know
anything of tongues
as we hid behind
barren blackberry bushes.
Innocence grew there,
barely even sun-kissed.
Was it supposed to sting?
Because it did.
I didn't kiss a man again
until I was 25.

The first time I kissed a girl,
I was 15,
and then 16,
and then 17,
and then 18.
It was so different.
So much softer, fruitful.
It felt…better.
Almost right.
But it still stung.

And instead of listening to my body,
I jumped straight into the brambles.
Ripping my skin open on thorns,
trying to find what was wrong with me.
So hungry for answers.
It took 30 years for that fruit to ripen
into the realization that there was
actually nothing wrong with me at all.
It was the sweetest juice
to ever stain my lips.
I just wish I had tasted it
a little sooner.

I Am A Woman – Jillian Calahan (she/her/they)

I am more than my uterus.
I am more than just a time capsule.
Born of the past
and holding the future in my belly.
I am a Woman.

I am more than my breasts.
I am more than a cup size.
My worth is measured
by what's IN my chest
not what's ON it.
I am a Woman.

I am more than my hips.
I am more than an hourglass figure.
I am less curves and more cliffs.
These edges were not made
for anyone else's hands
but were sharpened for those
who just cannot help themselves.
I am a Woman.

I am more than my vagina.
I am more than your personal
playground slip n' slide.
I am more than just a portal
for your pleasure.
My pleasure matters too.
And my hands know
just where to find it.
I am a Woman.

I am more than my cervix.
And it's spelled C-E-R-V-I-X
not SIR-VIX,
so you can keep your man-made laws
out of and off of my body.
I am a Woman.

I am more than my clitoris.
You would know that
if you could find it.
I am a Woman.

I am more than my labia.
So when I say "read my lips"
I'm not talking from my hips.
Maybe it's time we change that phrase
to read my teeth.
I am a Woman

I am more than my ovaries.
I am more than the hormones they carry.
The same hormones that make me
such a "raging bitch"
are the same hormones of my arousal.
You don't get to hate them half the time
and fuck them the other half.
I am a Woman.

So when you look at me
what do you see?
A baby factory?
A pleasure center?
A housewife?
A whore?
Or do you see Me?

I am a Woman.
If you see anything less
then you are blind.

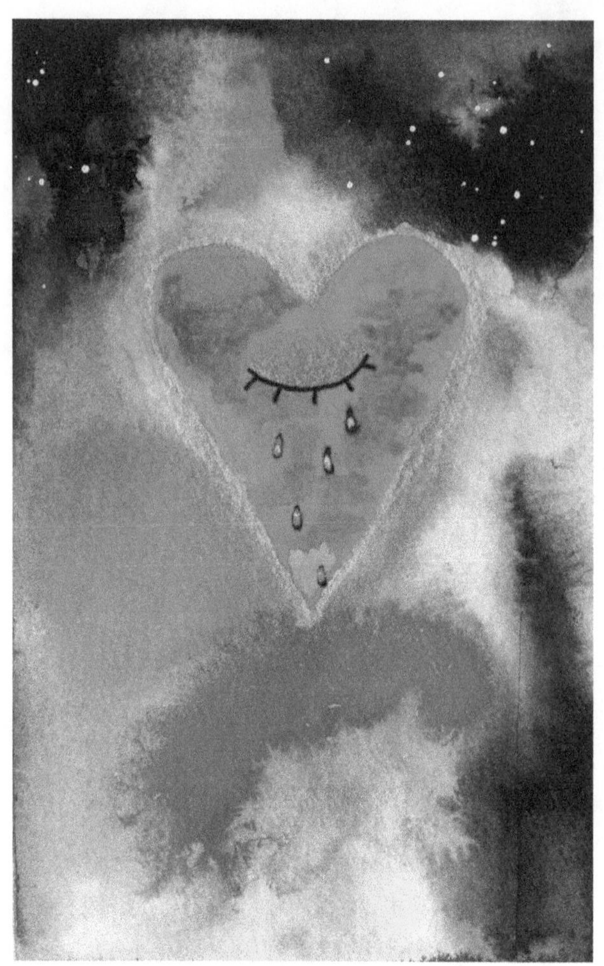

Wounded – Annie McCormick (they/she)

Cage – Annie McCormick (she/they)

Word Problems – L.M. Cole (she/they)

I can't quantify this queerness
in algorithms you can parse
but I'm carbon-based baby
compress me to conformity

fold me smaller in swansong
and airplane angles because
the shapes I make myself take
more space than this paper holds

left to my own pressure I could
dive into dreaming—leg folded
like can opener operatics into clear
conscious decision to be whatever

shrug this off like peeling an apple
but you should know the core
of this is just as bitter as your
mouth when you say *they*

1912 – DC Diamondopolous (she/her)

"Women and children first! Women and children first!"

A brandy snifter in one hand, a cigar in the other, I am alone as I watch people rush about on deck from the comfort of my leather chair in the first-class smoking room. It's past midnight, the lights flicker, but I am ruthlessly serene, for I did not overcome my childhood in the slums of the East End to drown in the freezing Atlantic water.

Second-class is where I belong, but who's to care now? When faced with death, we're all in the same boat.

Perhaps you've heard of me, Julian Grey, or seen my name on music hall marquees from Belfast to London.

I've made an enviable living as a comic, mimic, dancer, and acrobat. But what has brought me my greatest fame, and why I set sail on the Titanic to New York at the request of vaudeville manager, William Hammerstein, is my unfathomable ability to juggle five balls with my feet.

I put my cigar into an ashtray and set down the glass. Twisting the ends of my mustache, I am resolved about what I'm to do next, for I've never been one to pass up an opportunity.

I rise. The ship lurches. Poker chips, chess pieces, and tumblers fall on the floor. With my walking stick, I whack them away and stagger toward the door.

The ship creaks, a slow back and forth. The vessel tilts. I balance myself between the doorway.

The corridor is empty.

I open the door to a first-class suite. What finery, such elegance. There's a diamond stickpin and a ruby ring on the mahogany dresser. Did I mention that I am also a thief? I drop the stickpin and ruby ring into my coat pocket. I open the armoire and glide my hand over the dresses until I choose one.

If costumed in one lady's attire, I might draw attention, so I open the door to the next cabin.

"Excuse me, Sir," I say. A man holds a whiskey bottle in one hand and a Bible in the other. "Are you not going on deck?"

"Leave me be young man."

I shut the door.

The next room is charming, even as the furniture slides to the wall, with peacock patterns on overturned chairs, an electric fireplace, a vanity fit for Sarah Bernhardt. Stumbling, I open a chest of drawers, grab undergarments, and a scarf.

What I need is a warm coat, ladies' boots, and a hat. The lights go off, then on. I must hurry.

I enter a suite across the hall.

The room is in shambles. The dresser is on its side, a chair on its back. I throw the clothes on the bed and go to the trunk and take out a winter coat, lace-up boots, and a hat with a feather.

What I am about to do may seem shameful.

I sit on the edge of the bed next to the heap of clothes and remove my coat, then my tie and collar. My brother, may he rest in peace, comes to mind as I unbutton my shirt.

The binding is tight around my chest, and I begin to unfasten. Charles, was more than a brother, a father (I continue to unwind) to me, a motherless devil-rat, five years to his twelve. The bandage is off. My breasts are revealed.

I remove my trousers and drawers and pull the padding from between my legs. At a young age, Charles dressed me as a boy—*You'll be safer, and we can make a shilling or two.* We performed on street corners and in taverns, and as I grew and girls liked me, I liked them back. I am not an impersonator like the popular music hall drags. I am a man, and I've made the best of my oddity.

Naked, I dress.

Perfumes from the clothes make my eyes water. I put my wallet, cuff links, and stolen jewelry into the pocket of the woolen coat and squeeze my feet into the boots.

There is a strangeness to it, and I feel an utter distaste, the way the undergarments rustle and swish. Above the dresser is a mirror. I put on the hat and cover my short hair but leave a fringe that falls over my forehead. The mustache, I peel off and put in my pocket.

Pinching my cheeks, the way I've seen my lovers do, I leave the way I came and go to the deck.

Such chaos and panic. A man says good-bye to his wife and son as a lifeboat is lowered. Their cries provoke pity.

"Is there room?" I ask in a feminine voice.

"No, Miss," a crew member shouts. "Might be on the other side."

My unease mounts. I hurry among the crowd. My air of detachment collapses as I shove aside men and go around the stern. A lifeboat hangs from the davits.

"Women and children first!"

It's mayhem. Men implore their families to board, promising everything will be all right. From their shabby clothes, it's easy to see they're from steerage.

"What do we have here?" a shipmate yells. He removes a shawl and a scarf from the head of a man trying to board. "Josser."

A woman has the vapors and faints in her husband's arms.

A crowd gathers by a lifeboat hanging from the derricks. Men step aside as I make my way through.

Before me is a woman and her three daughters. Their tattered clothes arouse my sympathy. I slip the ruby ring into the woman's coat pocket.

"Come on, Miss," a deckhand says. He takes my arm and helps me into the boat.

Other than the two in command of rowing, I am the only man.

I dismiss any charge that I am a coward. Be that as it may, it will forever be a blessing, an irony indeed, that what saved me was the hand I was dealt.

1957 – DC Diamondopolous (she/her)

Welcome to The Shady Lady, a queer bar in San Pedro, California, across the railroad tracks, near the docks, in a back alley off Harbor Street. It's a raunchy hole-in- the-wall dive where dykes and drag queens hang. So you didn't think they mixed? Well, think again Daddy-O. Over there, slouched against the juke box, listening to Gogi Grant croon "The Wayward Wind," is Stormy, a big broad-shouldered butch who flirts with anyone who has tits and a pussy. Cigarette clamped to the side of her pouty James-Dean-like lips, she can talk, play pool, and switch-blade her way out of a fight, and the L&M never moves a lick. Her hair is greased with pomade and combed up on the sides with a pompadour rising like a tidal wave from her forehead. On the outside Stormy appears cool, but on the inside her stomach is doing wheelies. You see, a bust is about to happen, and she knows it.

Stormy yanks the jukebox plug from the wall. "It's the fuzz!" she shouts.

The teeny-weeny dance floor empties. The pool table is abandoned. Everyone scatters to small wooden tables and bar stools.

Stormy struts to the center of the room. "If the man rounds us up, fight back, you dig?"

"No sweat," someone answers.

Across the room, under the exit sign, meet VaVoom, a six-foot-five drag queen in stiletto heels raising her height to a near sky-scraping altitude. She wears a floral skirt with mesh petticoats, a black low-cut blouse, and a choker of fake pearls just below her Adams apple. Her short, Italian-styled wig is from Max Factor of Hollywood, and her layers of false eyelashes from Ohrbach's. She holds a cue stick like a ball bat. No way is VaVoom going to let Johnny Law give her the royal shaft.

Blue and maroon vice cars surround the seedy bar. Parked outside the lonely hideaway, the Black Mariah waits to haul off the sickos.

A gust of fish and gasoline swooshes in through the entrance. It's another night in the city where the heat gets their kicks hassling stompers, fems, and swishes.

"Okay motherfuckers, let's go. The freak show's over and the paddy's outside," a cop shouts.

"Didn't you get your pay-off?" a queen with a falsetto voice asks.

"Shut-up."

VaVoom hits the breakers.

Blackout!

Crash! Boom! Bam! Pop!

The Shady Lady turns into a blind noise of sticks swooshing, pool balls cracking, and feet scuffling. A flashlight cuts across the ceiling like a search-light at a movie premiere, but this ain't no movie. This is where dreams turn to pulp.

A fist slams Stormy in the back. "Ohh," she moans.

A stick strikes a skull.

A scream freeze-frames the moment.

It's our heroine VaVoom, holding the bloody cue. She shoves open the back door, swings the pole across the face of the cop guarding the exit and knocks him to the ground.

"Ahh," he cries and covers his broken nose.

VaVoom grabs Stormy. "Follow me."

"Where to?" Stormy asks.

"Hush-hush," Vavoom says. "It's very confidential." She pulls off her heels and sprints down the back street like Elroy "Crazylegs" Hirsch.

Stormy grips her cigarette between thumb and forefinger and flicks it away. She bolts after VaVoom.

Under a full moon, they run past cargo crates and pallets. The stink of diesel and garbage hangs in the air. The two escapees turn the corner at a cannery and dart alongside the Port of Los Angeles. Lights from Terminal Island flicker across the harbor. To the south, oil derricks and wells pump in an urban field of dinosaur spiders in 3-D. They both know what happens if caught—booked, fingerprinted, their names listed in the Daily Breeze under perverts. Lives ruined.

Stormy catches up to the towering drag queen. "Where the hell are we going?"

"To my boat," she says in a high-pitched breathy pant. "It's fabulous."

"You have a boat?"

"I dock in Long Beach," the transvestite says, gulping air. Her wig slips. She tugs it forward with one hand while dangling the straps of her heels with the other. "And sail here." She hurries toward the wharf.

Stormy charges after.

VaVoom runs down the pier to a small, wooden cabin cruiser and unties the rope. She lifts her skirt and long legs over the edge and steps into the boat. It rocks. Water ripples and gurgles. She opens the door to the cabin and disappears inside.

Stormy climbs into the boat. The cruiser laps from side to side. The door creaks back and forth.

"C'mon. Let's split," VaVoom's voice dips an octave. She fires up the engine.

Stormy swings open the door and steps inside. The crossdresser sits at the helm with her back to her. The queen's wig and stilettos are on the table. She runs a large hand over her crewcut, then peels off the blanket of eyelashes.

The big butch sits beside her partner in crime and lights a cigarette.

VaVoom powers the craft away from the dock and heads toward Long Beach.

"Thanks," Stormy says around the filter of her L&M.

VaVoom wipes her lipstick off with a tissue. She turns.

Stormy's cigarette falls to her lap. "Mr. Hazzelrigg!" she says, staring into the face of her tenth-grade math teacher.

"It's good to see you again, Mary Louise."

There Was No Aslan In My Closet – Beni Tobin (she/they)

I ran to my closet, flung open the wide wardrobe
doors and scrambled between the too-tight shelves.
Fit, fit, fit, I whispered, pushing past
dresses, coats, jumpers, and overalls,
all the clothes meant to make me feel
like I belonged.

I listened for Mr. Tumnus's hoofbeats
and sleigh bells. Sequined nylon brushed my cheek. I flinched!
My suit coat; like Turkish Delight: sweet,
tempting treat, covered in magic,
bewitchment meant to change my heart,
make me a Prince.

I looked for Narnia, clung to the old myth
promising me love, unyielding in spite of transgression.
There was no Aslan in my closet;
only me, crying tears of shame
for being Susan or Edmund:
too unworthy.

Do You Believe in Fairies? – Beni Tobin (she/they)

There They Are, Darlings:
Peter Pansexual,
The Lost Not-A-Boy
Who Never Realized
She/They Grew Up Too Soon
Until The Crocodile Tears
Flooded Their First Apartment.

They Ran Away From Home
The Day They Were Reborn, Past
The Mermaid Lagoon
And The Corner Saloon:
Ten Hours South And
Straight On To Mourning
A Childhood Filled With Expectations.

But They Are Not, After All,
A Lost Not-A-Boy,
They Are A Found One.
Now They Strut Proudly,
Flaunt Their Pixie Cut With Panache,
And Crow With A Strap-On
Cock-A-Doodle-Dooooo...

You Want To Meet Them?
First, Ask Yourself This:
Do You Believe In Fairies?
Because They Do,
And They Are,
And They Would Love
To Meet You Too.

my body's messenger – Haven Rittershofer-Ongoco (they/them/siya)

I write this as you rest on my temples
a subtle reminder that you are always with me
i find comfort in your familiarity
although we are often at odds and tensioned

you first asserted your irrevocable presence in 2014
confined me to a bed for the better part of 6 months
surfaced what i buried

i hated you, at first
you took away everything i was
    no more soccer, school, extracurriculars
    not even the internet, books, or conversations
    no more victories and celebrations with teammates,
    no more studying and aced exams,
    no more catholic confirmation duties,
i couldn't help around the house
    make my friends laugh
    feel the euphoria of pushing my body and mind to their limits
just darkness. and you. and me.

me?

when you took everything away, what of me was left?
you made me sit in my mind. isolated. but i wasn't alone.
hello, shame.
    the feeling of dis-ease when church leaders talked about the "women's" body—my body —as a
        "temple" to keep sacred for men
    that thing that crawled in my gut when my teammates made homophobic comments
    that act of convincing myself that i actually enjoyed kissing my cis, het boyfriend
    that weapon that killed the butterflies in my chest after a compliment from a pretty girl
you changed time for me
you desecrated that lifeline I—we (me and shame)—depended on to keep those truths hidden
now time passed not by days or activities, but by doctor's faces and colors of pills and intensity of
    side-effects
all in an attempt to quell you
and return me to who i was—should be

you see, years before you came to me, I had locked away a secret
a whisper so fragile that i thought i could tuck it in the folds of my memories
something "wrong" to be lost under the mountain of "right"
in wake of your forced quiet, it became deafeningly loud
it shuddered my bones until it rippled through my throat:

I LIKE GIRLS

those words hung suspended in the space between the bedroom floor where i stood and my childhood
mirror
terrified to focus on my reflection
in that moment, you lessened
and time started again

years later, in college, you were still with me when i repeatedly broke my bones and tore my muscles
the scans were at times obvious and at others inconclusive
the best sports doctors would point to *stress* and *force* and *eating disorder*
but you knew this was not the full truth
and it eventually surfaced:

I AM TRANS

still years later, chest freshly carved and vessel injected with hormones
you manifested in new ways
SSRIs and therapy couldn't stop you
i thought you were going to drive me to the end
but my community gave me new tools
and i used them to listen, and let you in
you beckoned—no demanded—i be in right relation with my own body, the land, spirit, and others
you showed me the way
towards transforming my conditions of harm

i was taught to eradicate, expel, drown out, push past you
now i know denying you abandons me
you, who refuses to be understood by the profession i trained in to control you (biomedical engineering)
you are the reason i know myself today

thank you, pain.

as i finish this writing, your weight on my temples has lessened
a sign you needed to be acknowledged
we needed to be held

i dream of a reality where we do not bury our pain
but hold it and ask it what needs tending
i hope this tending happens not alone but collectively
for the messages of pain can extend beyond the false confines of our skin
and lead us towards the truths we've known all along
but have been conditioned to forget

skin – Haven Rittershofer-Ongoco (they/them/siya)

i used to abandon my skin to feel ok
it's recognition prickled and bristled
so i burrowed deep into my flesh
over time i built insulation
materials sourced from false truths
this ensured
sensations could not reach me
i suffocated

i tore two gaping holes
an attempt to get the filling out
i must have missed some
remnants still wriggle and tingle
my brain severs the connection to forget they're there
but then i forget who i am
and who others are to me
and it's easier to let go

i try to take the pieces out
but it's hard to find them
they slither from my scars without warning
leap from my sockets and cloud my vision
crawl to the tips of my fingers and buffer reception
just when i think i know them
they storm back inside my gut
where the shame and desire for control live
then re-emerge in a new shape
they're tricky

i am extracting morsels slowly
catching the tail ends as they squirm away
parasites feeding off my synaptic transmissions
distorting my consciousness
leaving me to decipher between what is sharp
and what is tender

i won't give up
until every fragment is removed
doused in flames

ignited by transcestors
liberators
abolitionists
friends
hope
poured from my molten core

i refuse to abandon it any longer
my largest organ
for binding with it is communing with my vessel
entwining with the earth
it is healing all that is past
being in what is now
dreaming of what will come
it is opening vulnerable pores
to absorb the sun and the chemicals
and all that is raw and imperfect and perfect

i was disillusioned to believe
it is barrier to keep me safe
lies told by those who sold me the insulation
then profited off my dissonance
they are wrong
it is the conduit
through which all life passes

i see elements conducted through it
my power is harnessed at our interface
out to in
in to out
where they meet
is where i am whole
is where i am home

i feel my cells rejoice at this acknowledgement
finally they are known
soak it in they say
let it out they cry
this is all they ever wanted

i will not abandon my skin
for then i abandon everything

bloom where planted– Haven Rittershofer-Ongoco (they/them/siya)

i am figuring out how to bloom where planted
a lot of me wants to escape

this is where i was raised on stolen lands
this is where i was complicit in and subjected to violence under westernization, capitalism, colonialism, cis-hetero-patriarchy, and white supremacy
this is where i was conditioned to believe that being a biomedical engineer would help people live a "life worth living"
this is where i was lied to and denied access to my true self
this is where i pursued gender affirming care and receive medical and legal trauma
this is where i have harmed folks and fumbled into accountability
this is where i have been harmed and assaulted by members of my own "community"
this is where i feel lost and isolated and unable to fully receive though surrounded by queer and trans folks

this is where i choose to stay
to put down roots
to receive nourishment from the soil
to immerse myself in symbiotic relationships with the land and others
to stop striving 'for' and begin breathing, existing, struggling, decolonizing, living, imagining 'with'

i dream of building a pod and a chosen family rooted in transformative, loving, and healing justice
i dream of generative connections exchanging care and creativity and vulnerability
i dream of supporting the development of crisis intervention, safety, and justice practices outside of the state
i dream of using my privileges and experiences to create spaces where others can unleash their authenticity and uplift collective liberation

what dreams keep you where you are planted?

Digital drawing on a white background. An abstract depiction of the ylang-ylang flower, a native plant of the Philippines with medicinal properties.

collective dreaming – Haven Rittershofer-Ongoco (they/them/siya)

Digital drawing of a black open-faced book with outlines in rainbow colors. A pink sword emerges from the center pages flanked by fire and water. Rainbow drips from the spine to feed into a heart below.

This drawing was created as the emblem for the "Collective Dreaming" open mic night that is hosted monthly by the Transgender Health and Wellness Center.

We introduced the open mic space this way after the Club Q tragedy: Dreaming and storytelling have been used by our transcestors passed and liberators present for remembrance, survival, healing, and connection. In her short story, *The Book of Martha*, Octavia Butler posits that one solution to save humanity from self-destruction and move us towards peace, is dreaming—visceral, vivid, pleasurable, inescapable dreams. Sharing our individual dreams and holding one another's stories is an act of intimacy that nurtures us against the harm we face. Collective Dreaming is a TRANSformative response to violence.

Let's show them that we will not forget our radical legacies.
That they will not take away our divine right to dream and to love.
That in the wake of relentless violence, we will only become more devastatingly liberated.

what makes a person non-binary? – riel fuqua (they/them/theirs)

how can you define the undefinable
the knowing and the unknowing
the invariable and the malleable
the relinquished and the contained
the divine and the ostracized?
the incomparable and the incomprehensible
the center and the core?

what makes a person non-binary?
i don't know, ask.
ask them, these unfenced souls within
vessels blown pasture wide
these kin of universality
these folks with an x
these non-conforming adorned siblings
of both prism and spectrum
these presenters of fresh style and funky earring collections
these creators of spotify playlist love language
and chipped nail polish
these everydayers with everyday things on their everyday minds
these extra-extraordinaries

for whom there is no mold
no certain way
no instruction manual
no "for dummies" book
for whom there is no assigned pronoun to pronounce
for whom there is no singular song
but rather symphonies
themes and variations
unbridled, beautiful understanding
mixed with a fusion of misunderstood ears
and airpods with low batteries
and google searches
and misgendering from teachers
and analog thinking
and the unwritten laws of either or
instead of the blissful civil act of and.

what makes a person non binary?
everything
nothing
some
all
little
much.

you cannot ask
children birthed
of this effervescent
omnipresent universe
what qualifies
them
as an
experience

sappho's time– riel fuqua (they/them/theirs)

will i love you in coffee grounds and cast-iron skillet breakfasts?
will you whisper to me, full of sugar and all things allure
- "*yes, please*" -
while i thumb you open
gentle
aware
careful
as there can be not a crease
not a dog ear
not a single page skipped from all of your pages?

i want to take you to visit eden entirely
you angel you
staring back at me
as if there is more of your universe
you want to thread my fingertips
and walk me through—
your caverns unexplored
unless you decide to let me
and i would blush
at such an honor

is it pinot grigio or cabernet sauvignon that you want to pair with our dinner tonight?
on the way home,
i will stop by the flower shop on the corner
and think about the folding that needs doing
and the open air on my mouth

you are a home in a house-dress
you sparkle like prism
and sun spillings
on the carpet

the drone of our bath water running
the cookies that are baking in the oven
cat toys scattered on the hardwood floors that need sweeping

now it is morning time
and your mouth is fixed for some butter on brioche
it is winter time
and you borrow my snow boots to go check the mail
(that don't lace up quite right)
we are on sappho's time
and there are little laugh lines
in the creasing of my eyes

i fold you up and keep you in my billfold
to show to all of the birds

Subliminal – Jean Woodleigh (she/her)

Shame spreads like spores and *fear*

Poking at my sanity and my decisions: *ideas*
living in our female heads and in the images
on the walls and on our lips,
warping, wavering, like a distorted mirage,

nonetheless real

I think:
if I'm not the best I'm not equal
and if I don't want to, I'm selfish
and if I waver, I'm not generous
and if my love is not unconditional—
and if I feel—

It's so bad I cannot speak.

And so I wear it like spores on my skin, microscopic:
The things I should be and the things I am,
The things that are and the things I want,
The things other people see,
The real and the unreal, *insanity*
embedded roots burying down
Blurred within the woven net that is the world.

Bloody White Veil – Nazmi Shaikh (she/her)

she waited 5 hours that night
crestfallen on the porch
being reduced to an amorphous leader
of the house that she swore she'd be bound to
when the veil spun with fragments of her freedom was put on her
she put her faith in your humbug
thinking she'd be saved from her family
her blurred periphery prevented her to see the deceit I saw right through you
I know you're knee-deep in filth
she slept 2 hours that night
quivering on the floor with pain
weeping on an open grave
unraveling her mistakes in the past life
holding out her hand for you – a chance
your refusal was a common visitor to her
just like dewy marks on your collarbone
her eyes glisten with denial as she looks up to you
cleaning your knees with the remains of her veil

La Llorona – Daniella Navarro (she/her)

Who am I
without this thieving grief?
I don't know if I can ever stop writing
poems about you.

Who am I
when the world is?
When the world isn't? You, my black hole
universe. Unspoken absence

at the family table. Your last breath
in reverse sucking the gravity
out of laughter. Flinging
my tears to the sky.

I thought I was capricious,
but that was before I met the ghost
of you. I am La Llorona
now. Brother,

why does your memory bay
louder than lonely
whales?
Than all the lost children?

poltergeist – Daniella Navarro (she/her)

I imagine
the poltergeist in my home is you
harmlessly dropping chips
off of the untouched
shelf, hiding bits
and bobs, a thump
in the middle of the night.
These strange
occurrences should not bring me comfort,
but I already scream
single, compacthurricanes. Drink well-wishes
in the morning. Trumpet the fire in
                                                            -to ash.
Touchridges of stones
I've already lost. Show the cats
that this bird is just flyingsilence.
Tell walls I hate
theirsmiles. Welcomebaggage
of saltwater and trees. Make friends
withvinegar ants. Bark
at spinning books. Prematurelysnuff
a burningrecord. Exist
as tamales in a can. Pop my-
-self in themicrowave.

Throwoutmyextrahands.Peelthespaghetti.Obscene
themirrors.Candletheframes.Danceongummyhorses.
Wifiaroundthepiano.Skipchihuahuasonthemilk.Sing
inthekeyofpuppets.Laughthemadness.Bidfarewellto
thehoneycombrainbows.

This is me not knowing how
to miss you without losing

my sanity.

I Choose What Grows Here – Chelsey Hudson (she/her)

an awakening – Kayla Porth (she/her)

i remember the first male gaze
sliding slick down my body
twelve years old with grasshopper's legs
those groping winks hurled my way
sprouted hives in my chest

i remember the way shining white
hallways echoed my shame:
the shoulder | the thigh
the tampon | the strap
the cleavage | the midriff | the fingertip rule
the shape | of my body | does not belong | in school

i remember conveyor belt origami
the art of folding feminine surface area
pretzels twist now in my shoulders
i sit tight-lipped on buses and
cross-legged in conference rooms

i haven't been the same since
the first perfect retouched hand
reached up from a glossy page
tracing my lips, twirling a finger—
a lock of my hair—and suddenly
jerking down hard

my cheek crashing to the world's curb

the saliva of throbbing strangers

the still-sweet tears on my face

capsule – Kayla Porth (she/her)

how to identify the gender curse:

1. mind-bending acrobatics to land: self-love
2. decades to forget: the first feeling of eyes they glide

the slope:
your back
3. a full room, a half-moment: size you up score your value
your aesthetic appeal
your humanity
a quick wink
hollow 10-point scale
4. one flock of fingers
a shrieking half-moment
the sinking
your psyche
5. decades
to say it aloud

6. mind flying back to twelve
knowing you'd done something terrible standing there: taking up space

7. everything is up for scrutiny
it keeps you busy, keeps you unsure
of the way you move the way you make this world keeps you off kilter and scanning the room for acceptable beauty hues | beauty do's | beauty lewd

8. your dreams hosted by a botox bombshell she says *i'm here to help*
she assesses the mess
and lathers up
massaging mania into your skull
pressing it in with holy water
and hell fire
you struggle awake
9. but already feverish circles
frantic venn diagrams
are forming deep below the skin

a history – Kayla Porth (she/her)

listen to me, beloved
embolden your lips
No is punch-perfect

neglect
to give a fuck
about a thigh gap

you must muster the pain and rage of the millions before you

who have been caged birds concubines corsets and witches
bound feet bowing like cats we have stood in dirt floor kitchens
we have died as damsels and dowries and mutilated flowers
blurred reflections of bloated bodies in lakes and breeders

we've squat low soaked fluorescent in grocery aisles
wailing babies tumbling out between our spread knees

we have been catches and trophies and conquests
we have turned to stone with thin silver bands
we have been painted pink still wet in the womb

my god, you must remember the thousands before you, you
must feel them crawling up your ribs
the bright apple juice rivers coursing wildly down their chins

rebirth – Kayla Porth (she/her)

still we rise
the past laden in our ankles
the future: the marrow of our spines

we bend to lift daughters
delta dances on our shoulders
we are stripping away the heavy folds
we are pulling back the thousand veils:
like twisting soft bodies of doves
they fall slip-slow to the earth
the chains the cages the scarlet vowels
blistering in our chests:

they drop

remember the best of us have not yet come
O we are carpets for their feet

the golden flames of our crowns cut the bursting belly of the sun

we open our arms to catch them:
our ever-spreading futures

Tread Lightly – Alice Carroll (she/her)

How do you grieve?

Where do you place this weight?

Who put lead where lungs were supposed to be?

I'm forced to my knees

A pittance for sweet air

I am afraid the way I have to live might momentarily paralyze an unsuspecting passerby

So I try to offer feasible doses to those who don't paint their pity with a sellsword's compassion

And the girl in the glass is silent

Bloodstains mirror my reflection as I grab the Windex

Knowing they'll seep through any substance that carries my likeness

I think I've been loved before

I know it

There's something that fills the corners that sometimes scatters the shadow

So I politely ask that you knot your laces and veer from my path

You don't know how to walk on broken glass

ABOUT THE CONTRIBUTORS

- Abigail Guidry (she/her) is an archivist, writer, and photographer from Louisiana. She writes for Artists' Book Reviews and lives with two cats in Madison, Wisconsin.

- AJ Schnettler is a nonbinary, multi-racial photographer and printmaker born and raised on the South Shore of Long Island. They decided to get a new perspective on life and education by moving to the West Coast to pursue their Bachelor of Fine Arts degree in Photography with a minor in Printmaking from the San Francisco Art Institute in 2019. Their work is based around what one does to provide self-acceptance. They work through identity or the space surrounding them; how to feel at peace overcoming negative, social, and cultural pressure. Most recently discussing mental health emphasizing anxiety, body dysmorphia, and social standards. Their printmaking work confronts the topics of depression and anxiety. They have received the Silver Artist Award from ArtAscent Magazine, have work in the permanent collection of the Kruizenga Art Museum, and are featured in Ikouii Creative's second edition of their book Inside Their Studio: Deaf and Disabled Artists Reshaping the Arts. They can be found in the directories of Visionary Art Collective, Now Be Here Art, and Asian American Women Arts Association.

- Alexandria Piette is a resident of her birthplace, Grand Rapids, Michigan, with her mother and foster siblings. She is the indie author of *The Blazing Heart of a Moonlight Arsonist*. She enjoys literature and poetry, viewing the numerous seasons of Supernatural on repeat, and caring for her dog, Bentley, and hellion kittens, Rue and Winston. You can find them on Instagram, @alexandriapiette, @apbooksart, and Twitter, @alexandriapiett.

- Alice Carroll lives in the midwest and writes poetry. Sometimes, she gets paid for it.

- Amelie Honeysuckle is a student at the University of Colorado Boulder and made her debut in poetry with her book, "What Once Was An Inside Out Rainbow." Amelie is a lover of words and believes that one of the most beautiful ways to colorfully create is through the art of words. Amelie loves finding unconventional beauty in her environment and thrives through writing love poetry for her people.

- Ananiah has always been a writer ever since she could write, however, only recently has she ventured into the world of professional writing. Her work has previously been published with Wingless Dreamers, Querencia and more. Ananiah is an avid reader. She reads books from all genres and particularly enjoys reading YA fiction, philosophical works and fantasy. Ananiah loves cats more than anything else in the world and has befriended many over the years. Mia is Ananiah's furry orange companion that keeps her company as she stays up past midnight engrossed in reading.

- Annie McCormick (they/she) is a nonbinary artist and educator living in Fort Worth, Texas. Their preferred mediums for visual art include watercolors and inks that allow colors to blend and flow in ways that can be influenced but not fully controlled. Annie hopes to offer honest glimpses of the depths and heights of intimate personal experience, inviting viewers to connect her images with the light and shadow of their own lives.

- Antonia Rachel Ward is an author of horror and Gothic fiction, based in Cambridgeshire, UK. Her short stories and poetry have been published by Blackspot Books, Kandisha Press, and Orchid's Lantern, among others. Her gothic horror novella, MARIONETTE, was published by Brigid's Gate Press in August 2022 and her second novella, ATTACK OF THE KILLER TUMBLEWEEDS! is forthcoming in May 2023. She is also the founder and editor-in-chief of Ghost Orchid Press. You can find her at antoniarachelward.com or on Twitter @antoniarachelw1 or Instagram @antoniarachelward.

- Beni Tobin (she/they) is a non-binary, pansexual writer living in California with their spouse, children, and dogs. Their experiences inform their writing as a parent, a member of the LGBTQIA+ community, and an apostate of evangelical Christianity. Their writing has been featured in the Motherly Collective, and they published their first poetry chapbook, "My Family Tree Caught Fire," through Bottlecap Press.

- Brooke is a queer poet from San Diego, California. Brooke started out their poetry career in the spoken word community in 2019 and has since then performed in cities such as Seattle, Phoenix, Los Angeles and Las Vegas. They have also had the opportunity to merge their passion for advocacy and the arts by speaking at human rights rallies and abortion rights fundraisers. They have previous work published in Poet's Underground Anthology Volume I. When Brooke isn't writing, you can find them in the mountains with their pup and a dead car battery, hoping everything works itself out.

- Che Flory (they/them) is primarily an actor and director for the stage, which is their current focus at North Dakota State University. They write across genre with a focus on playwriting. Their plays are all accessible on the New Play Exchange. They have also been published in *The Offing*. Instagram: k.flory

- Chelsey Hudson is submitting a visual art piece focused on women's reproductive rights. She is a 32 year old mother of 3 children, who resides in New York. She is passionate about the women's right to choose when it comes to abortion laws. Her belief is that all women's bodies are like gardens. The woman who possesses the garden is the only one who has the right to choose what grows in it. Thank you for your consideration.

- Christina D. Rodriguez is a Latinx poet, entrepreneur, and woman of tech from New York, currently living in Chicago. Her poems have appeared in *Tupelo Quarterly, Yes, Poetry, Rust + Moth, Satin Soulbits*, and elsewhere; her work has also been published in various anthologies. Christina has received awards for the Frost Place Conference on Poetry and Winter Tangerine's Catalyze Self-Revolutions workshop. She has performed at the Chicago Public Library, The New York Poetry Festival, and Columbia College Chicago. She is a board member of the Chicago Writers Association as the organization's social media manager and poetry editor for CWA's *The Write City Magazine.* She is also a contributor to the Instagram poetry book club, Can We Discuss Poetry. *Knees in the Garden* (Querencia Press, 2023) is her first collection. To learn more about Christina, visit her at crodonline.info or @poemlust on Instagram.

- Claire is a Scottish poet based in the south of Spain. She is the EIC and founder of The Wee Sparrow Poetry Press. She has had poetry published by a variety of indie presses and she was long-listed for the Erbacce Poetry Prize in 2021.

- Culkeeen (he, his,him) is a french creator trying to make art with his own two hands, broken pencils and outdated freewares. He painted and pasted things up all around the world. Most of his art is also derived into stickers which are traded worldwide.

- Dani Solace (they/he/she) is a queer author and illustrator. They currently reside and work in Oklahoma City. More of her writing can be found on his blog, poetrybysolace.com.

- Daniella Navarro is a part-time poet and full-time Hispanic American. She lives in Austin, TX, with Esmeralda, Juan Pablo, and Shane—two of whom are her cats, one of whom is her human boyfriend, but all of whom are house-trained. She started writing poems in the seventh grade and graduated from Texas State University with a bachelor's degree in creative writing. She works as an editor to provide a good life for her cats, but she hopes the five-day workweek is abolished once AI inevitably takes over. Instagram: @poetdaniella

- Dawn K. Wing is a Chinese American multi-disciplinary artist/ librarian based in St. Paul, MN. She earned her B.A. in Studio Arts and Art History at Wellesley College. Her creative interests include mixed media visual narratives, poetry, book arts, underrepresented histories and collective memory. For updates on Dawn's creative projects, visit www.waterpigpress.com.

- DC Diamondopolous is an award-winning short story, and flash fiction writer with hundreds of stories published internationally in print and online magazines, literary journals, and anthologies. DC's stories have appeared in: *Progenitor, 34th Parallel, So It Goes: The Literary Journal of the Kurt Vonnegut Museum and Library, Lunch Ticket,* and others. DC's recently released collection *Captured Up Close (20th Century Short-Short Stories)* has two Pushcart Prize nominated stories and one nominated for Best of the Net Anthology. Her first collection of stories was *Stepping Up.* She lives on the California coast with her wife and animals. dcdiamondopolous.com

- "Stop the world. And Melt" is from The Undeads- a Collection of Pink Zombie Rose Comics, written by Dia and illustrated by Beppi. Known only as "Beppi" in the comicpedia, no last name needed, the artist has worked in comics, textiles, sculpture and fine arts. She explores culture and experiments with form. Dia does the same in her work. The author was a decade into Pink Zombie Rose when she realized she was writing a series of graphic novels. She went straight to Beppi. To learn more about PZR https://www.instagram.com/pinkzombierose/ www.pinkzombierose.com —To learn more about Beppi, https://www.instagram.com/beppiisbert www.circleofevil.com —To learn more about Dia - www.diavangunten.com (Dia is EIC of Cream Scene Carnival, @creamscenecarnival. Beppi is a curator for the magazine.)

- dre levant has a fierce passion for writing, their cat sochi, and veggie subway sandwiches. with an eclectic style and vibrant voice, dre loves to write weird poems and make funky art. their work has been published in fifth wheel press, tiny spoon lit mag, dreamers creative writing, prometheus dreaming, and mistake house. for snippets of poetry and cat pics, follow @drethepiper on instagram and twitter.

- Duna Torres Martín (she/her) is a poet, writer, collagist and musician from Madrid, Spain. She has two poetry collections out, 'Limbo' and 'Desierto', as well as several contributions to various anthologies and zines, including '99% Chance of Magic'. Her work usually deals with health, LGBT+ issues, memory and relationships, and she loves collaborations.

- Emily Long (they/she) is a queer writer living in Denver, Colorado. A winner of the 2021 True Colors poetry prize with Vocal Media & Moleskine, Emily has also been published in Anti-Heroin Chic, Quail Bell Magazine, & Passengers Journal, among others. You can find Emily on Instagram at @emdashemi, or more likely, you'll find them paddleboarding, hiking, and climbing in the Rocky Mountains with their partner and rescue pup.

- Haven Rittershofer-Ongoco (they/them/siya) is a white-bodied, genderqueer human of mixed slavic/germanic and filipinx descent, passionate about helping the queer and trans community build the tools, capacity, and support to collectively bloom where they are planted. They do this through community organizing efforts around transformative justice and by practicing embodied tattoo artistry.

- Heather Meatherall is a poet from Canada. She finds a lot of inspiration from quotes, music and nature, as well as her own lived experiences. Heather is currently studying Computer Science at Ontario Tech University. You can find her on Instagram under the handle @heathermeatspoetry

- Isabelle Quilty (she/they) is a non-binary writer and poet from regional NSW, Australia. Most of their work is based around LGBTQ+ topics, working towards a greener future and works inspired by their South Asian ancestry. They've been published by a variety of magazines including *Spineless Wonders Queer as Fiction Anthology, Kindling and Sage, Mascara Literary Review and Demure Magazine.* They also have a bachelor's degree in the Creative Industries and love a good oat milk iced latte.

- Jean Woodleigh is an aspiring poet with a passion for whimsical words and forests by night. While writing has been her dream for as long as she can remember, she rediscovered poetry in 2020 during the pandemic. *Subliminal* is her first poem to be published.

- Jenny Benjamin is the owner of her freelance writing and editing business JB Communications, LLC. Over thirty of her poems have appeared in journals, including *DIAGRAM, South Carolina Review, Fulcrum, Baltimore Review, Chelsea*, and the *Crab Orchard Review*. Her first novel, *This Most Amazing*, was published in 2013 by Armida Books in Nicosia, Cyprus. Her poetry chapbook, *More Than a Box of Crayons*, was published by Finishing Line Press in February 2018. Her poetry chapbook, *Midway*, won second place in the 2017 No Chair Press contest and was published in April 2018. *Enhanced* and *Corrupted*, the first two books of her young adult, science fiction trilogy were published by Ananke Press (October 2021, July 2022). *Redeemed: Book Three of the Terrian Trilogy* is forthcoming in 2023. Her novel *Heather Finch* was published by Running Wild Press (June 2022). She lives in Milwaukee, Wisconsin with her three children and dog.

- Jen Schneider is a community college educator who lives, works, and writes in small spaces throughout Pennsylvania.

- Jess (she/her) is a musician-turned-writer and disability advocate from Australia. She has Ehlers-Danlos Syndrome, Fibromyalgia, Essential Tremor, and Pre-Menstrual Dysphoric Disorder. She is passionate about using her negative experiences in the healthcare field to help other members of the chronic illness and disability communities feel less alone, and empower them to practise fearless self-advocacy when necessary. You can see more of Jess' work on www.delicatelittlepetal.com or on Instagram @delicatelittlepages.

- Jillian Calahan (she/her/they) is a poet and short story writer from Seattle, Washington. When she's not writing you can find her in a bookstore, chilling with her 4 cats and 2 dogs, crafting, or taking too many pictures of pretty sunsets. You can find her work on Instagram @novamarie_poetry

- jomé rain is a writer and sex worker in her mid twenties, currently living between nyc and paris. she adores love, lust, and her puppy: scarlet.

- Julie Elefante is a nerdy, bi, Filipino American and the youngest and only girl of five second-gen kids. She developed her love of words as a speech therapy child with selective mutism and fell in love with her dad's storytelling as a way of healing, nurturing, and unifying. She studied humanities and architecture in college and is now an editor in the Arizona desert. One of her proudest achievements was creating a little zine company called rock scissors paper and spearheading an event called the 24-Hour Zine Thing.

- Julie Lee (she/her) is a Korean-American artist from Alabama working primarily in photography and collage. She holds a BFA (Bachelor of Fine Arts) from Carnegie Mellon University (CMU) and is residing in Pittsburgh, PA. Through the family album, her lens-based works explore themes of ancestry and the photograph as existential affirmation, with a particular focus on the matrilineal lineage that comes with her and the women around her. Her work has been exhibited in Woman Made Gallery, Columbia University's PostCrypt Gallery, the Curated Fridge, the Children's Museum of Pittsburgh, the Colorado Photographic Arts Center, Filter Space, the Associated Artists of Pittsburgh, and the Pittsburgh International Airport. Her work has also been featured in publications such as the Journal of Art Criticism, Yale University's Asterisk* Journal of Art and Art History, Hyperallergic, and Fraction Magazine.

- Kamilah Mercedes Valentín Díaz is a queer identifying caribeña. At a young age she moved from Puerto Rico to the U.S. with her family. This change came with many challenges, but also jump started her journey with literature, reading, and writing. As a poet and writer, she delves into matters of identity, bilingualism, revolution, mental health, nature, and decolonization. You can read more of her work in her first poetry collection, *Morivivi: To Have Died yet Lived.*

- Kayla Porth has been published in The South Carolina Review and Semantics and won The University of South Carolina's S.O.S. for HAITI poetry contest. After a decade hiatus building her career and raising her son, Kayla returns to poetry to reinvent herself. She is currently working on her first manuscript.

- K.G. Munro is an author and poet. Her poetry has been published in other outlets such as Poetry Potion, Oddball Magazine, Agape Review, Green Ink Magazine, Scarlet Dragonfly, FeversOfTheMind and many others.

- Korbyn McKale is a poet from Perry, Oklahoma. She earned her Bachelor's in Creative Writing at the University of Central Oklahoma. While at UCO, Korbyn worked as an assistant editor for the New Plains Review from 2020-2021. She self-published her first chapbook, For the Fragile Ones, in January of 2022, a compilation of uplifting poetry about self-love and appreciation of the world, from the cosmically wondrous to the beautifully mundane. Much of Korbyn's work is introspective and explores the fragility of life, the intricate tapestry of consciousness, womanhood, and the complexities of interpersonal relationships. You can keep up with her at KorbynMcKalePoetry.com.

- Lee Martínez Soto (they/ellx) is a published queer Chicanx poet and translator. Their work centers on mental health stigma: life with comorbid mental health diagnoses, finding accessible resources and competent specialists, and healing. The author self-published their first poetry anthology, Para los Locos in 2020. Additional publications include Chismosa Press vol 4 (2022), Chrysalis Literary Journal (2021), Life in the Time (2021), Chismosas Press vol. 3 (2020), Living Zine vol. 2 (2020), and Nuestras Voces with Massachusetts's College of Liberal Arts (2014).

- Native New Yorker LindaAnn LoSchiavo, a Pushcart Prize, Rhysling Award, Best of the Net, and Dwarf Stars nominee, is a member of SFPA, The British Fantasy Society, and The Dramatists Guild. Elgin Award winner "A Route Obscure and Lonely," "Concupiscent Consumption," "Women Who Were Warned," Firecracker Award, Balcones Poetry Prize, Quill and Ink, and IPPY Award nominee "Messengers of the Macabre" [co-written with David Davies], and "Apprenticed to the Night" [Beacon Books, 2023] and "Felones de Se: Poems about Suicide" [Ukiyoto, 2023] are her latest poetry titles.

- Linda M. Crate's works have been published in numerous magazines and anthologies both online and in print. She is the author of eleven published chapbooks, four full-lengths, and four micro-chaps. She has a novella, also, called *Mates* (Alien Buddha Publishing, March 2022).

- Lindsay Valentin is a lesbian writer and letterpress artist living and working in Los Angeles. She has written for magazines and publications such as *BUST, GO NYC, Odyssa*, and *Pink Pangea*. Her poetry focuses on the intrcate, spiritual workings of the creative mind and life, and making known those pieces of culture, including LGBTQ culture and experience, that may be lesser known.

- L.M. Cole is a Pushcart Prize-nominated poet residing in North Carolina. Her work has appeared or is forthcoming with Roi Fainéant, Corporeal, Messy Misfits, The Pinch Journal, The Bitchin' Kitsch and others. She can be found on Twitter @_scoops__

- Lucy Puopolo (she/her) is currently a high school junior based in Puerto Rico. She is a Kenyon Review Young Writer's Workshop alumna and has published work in *orangepeel*. She has a bothersome habit of thinking about writing more than effectively doing so.

- Madalyn R. Lovejoy (she/they) is a part-time barista and data analyst, studying Psychology and Gender, Women's, & Sexuality Studies at the University of Iowa. She spends time volunteering at the local Women's Resource and Action Center and playing D&D with her friends. They enjoy knitting, reading books that make them question humanity, and being out in nature. Forthcoming work will appear in *Boundless* Volume VII. They can be found anywhere @mad_lovejoy.

- Marianna Pizzini Mankle (she/her/hers) is a Montana native calling Nebraska home. Her writing can be found in *Kiosk, Writeresque Literary Magazine, Spoonie Press, New Note Poetry*, and more. She can be found watching reality TV or NCIS with her husband when she isn't writing.

- Marina Carreira (she/they) is a queer Luso-American poet artist from Newark, NJ. She is the author of Tanto Tanto (Cavankerry Press, 2022) and Save the Bathwater (Get Fresh Books, 2018). She has exhibited her art at Morris Museum, ArtFront Galleries, West Orange Arts Council, Monmouth University Center for the Arts, among others. She holds an MFA in Creative Writing and is pursuing a D.Litt. in Fine Arts and Media. Keep up with her at hellomarinacarreira.com.

- Marisa Silva-Dunbar's work has been published in The Bitchin' Kitsch, ArLiJo, Pink Plastic House, Sledgehammer Lit, Analogies & Allegories Literary Magazine. Her second chapbook, "When Goddesses Wake," was released in December, 2021 from Maverick Duck Press. Her first full-length collection, "Allison," was recently published by Querencia Press. You can find her on Twitter and Instagram @thesweetmaris. To check out more of her work go to www.marisasilvadunbar.com

- Mattie-Bretton Hughes is a disabled, nonbinary-trans writer from Detroit, Michigan. He writes poetry to explore his identity, his body, as well as mental health, trauma, intimate partner abuse, disability, addiction, and LGBTQ activism; mixed with a message of hope, self-acceptance and love. He is currently working on a chapbook, a full length manuscript of poetry, and a novel series of historical fiction focusing on themes ranging from LGBTQ, trauma, addiction, and dysfunctional family cycles. Mattie-Bretton also runs his own on-line writing group.

- Melissa Frederick has been working at writing for the past 35 years, through motherhood, chronic illness(es), and societal insanity. She earned Master's degrees from Iowa State University and Temple University. Her poetry and prose have appeared in numerous publications, including *Crab Orchard Review, DIAGRAM, Mid-American Review, Moon City Review, Muse/A Journal, Oxford Poetry*, and *Heron Tree*. Her poetry chapbook, *She*, was published by *Finishing Line Press* in 2008. Her work has also been nominated for the Pushcart Prize and the Best of the Net anthology. Follow her on Instagram at @missficklereader or on Mastodon at @missficklereader@mstdn.social

- Michele Zimmerman (she/her) is a Queer writer with a BA and an MFA in fiction from Sarah Lawrence College. Her work appears in Catapult's TINY NIGHTMARES: VERY SHORT TALES OF HORROR, POST ROAD, SUPERFROOT, and more. She is a winner of the FRACTURED LITERARY Anthology II Contest and the BLOOD ORANGE REVIEW 2021 Literary Contest. In the past she has been a SUNDRESS PUBLICATIONS Best of the Net nominee & a two-time finalist for the GLIMMER TRAIN Short Story Award for New Writers. By day, she edits and writes for a magazine about illumination and design. Find her at www.michelezimmerman.com.

- Mimi Flood is the author of Baby Blue (Bottlecap Press). She has been published in Dark Thirty Poetry Publishing, Querencia Press, The Graveyard zine, Scar Tissue Magazine, and Gypsophila. You can find her on Instagram Marigold_Jesus.

- Mo McMasters (they/them) is a a comic artist, illustrator, and storyboard artist based in Los Angeles. Their latest publication is "In the Eyes of the Shadow," a comic featured in After the End: A Post-Apocalyptic Comics Anthology, and their work has been in gallery shows at Junior High LA, Gallery Nucleus, Cartoon Network Studios, and Usagi NY

- Moriah Katz is a Black/Jewish writer. Her work explores the imprint of race, gender, and sexuality on the human experience, and can be found in Stellium Literary Magazine, The Queer26, just femme & dandy literary magazine, and more. She holds a degree in Literature from the University of California, Santa Cruz.

- nat raum (b. 1996) is a disabled artist, writer, and genderless disaster from Baltimore, MD. They're a current MFA candidate at the University of Baltimore and also hold a BFA in photography and book arts from the Maryland Institute College of Art. nat is also the editor-in-chief of fifth wheel press and the author of *you stupid slut,* as well as several chapbooks and photography publications. Past publishers of their writing include *Delicate Friend, Corporeal Lit,* and *trampset*. Find them online: natraum.com/links.

- Nazmi is an aspiring writer and a fervent fan of sneaking out of events expeditiously. She's currently pursuing BA in Psychology and when she isn't oscillating between writing and college, she's catering to her propensity of analyzing movies, tv shows and albums.

- Paris is a sophomore at the University of Oregon. He is an English major with a double minor in creative writing and classics, and spends his time editing for The Student Insurgent, a radical newspaper on campus. His previous publications include North Dakota Quarterly, and he has a poem forthcoming in Crow & Cross Keys. He spends his free time at the LGBTQ center on campus and doing open mics in the local community. You can find him on Instagram and Twitter @parisofthedark

- Rachel Coyne is a woman writer and painter from Lindstrom, Mn

- Rachel Mulder lives in Portland, Oregon, with her two cats, Opal and Tomasina. She was born in rural Wisconsin and when she was small she spent a lot of time sitting in the grass staring, obsessing about animals, watching cartoons and peeling her skin off. Now she makes drawings using a variety of media that often yield printmakerly textures - residual effects from earning her BFA in Printmaking at Milwaukee Institute of Art & Design in 2007. Encouraging others (and herself) to create/exist sincerely is a parallel passion of hers that braids itself into her visual work.

- Revika Sangamita (she/they) is weaving their portrait of being a queer poet, storyteller and artist while residing amidst New Delhi. She embraces her mental health issues, healing, hope, grief and self love through poetry. Usually dancing to the rhythm of her own beats and rarely cleaning the chaos. They can be positively found attending workshops in a zombie apocalypse. Their work has been featured in Live Wire India, Bloom Magazine, Graveyard Zine, Evoke & Echo Literary Magazine and several anthologies. She is also a staff poet at Outlander Zine. You can connect with them on Instagram @revikasangamita.

- riel fuqua (they/them/theirs) is a creative artist of many trades, each of them centering around the communicative art of storytelling. much of riel's work focuses on the mosaic of experiences they have had as a Black, queer person residing in the Deep South, including navigating interpersonal relationships, sentiments both big and small, childhood memories, the nostalgia for a reality before COVID-19, and the zest of Black, non-binary joy. riel's debut publication, "breathing in a black body" was featured in BLOOM's Spring 2020 zine publication entitled 'Race and Gender'. in addition to poetry, riel is an accomplished vocalist with several years of vocal performance training. their research interests include works by marginalized composers, African-American spirituals, the poetry of Langston Hughes, inclusivity in opera and musical theatre, transgender and non-binary voice pedagogy, mutual aid, sustainability for underprivileged communities, and gender studies. riel currently resides in florence, alabama, where they spend most of their time romanticizing the necessary mundane—nourishing, resting, connecting, and daydreaming—while they balance work at both a local university and an art museum.

- Roya Motazedian (they/them) is a nonbinary poet/writer born in the Netherlands, raised in England, and currently residing in Canada. Their parents were born and raised in Iran. While in their final year of an English BA, they have been writing poetry that revolves around their gender identity, ethnic/cultural identity, and what it truly means to be 20 in the 21st century.

- Ryan Jafar Artes (she/they) is an adoptee, activist, memoirist, poet, and self-published author. Their work includes *After Midnight* and *Friendship Zine,* with writing in anthologies published by *Capturing Fire Press, Prometheus Dreaming,* and the *BIPOC Writing Community*. Ryan hosts two events exclusively for adoptees, The Adoptee Open Mic and Let's Thrive Together, a generative writing workshop. They are pursuing a self created and designed MFA while writing poetry and memoir.

- S. Kavi is a South Indian American writer and artist. Her work involves exploration of South Indian culture, the beauty of nature, nostalgia, and healing. Her work appears most recently in antonym, Suspension Literary Magazine, Cordelia Magazine, The Firefly Review, and elsewhere.

- Sam Indigo Lydia Fern is a queer nonbinary trans woman, 25 years old, and a Taurus Rising. She is a white settler living on occupied ancestral and current Wintu homeland, colonially known as Redding, California. She likes plants, bugs, and systems, she is fascinated with tarot and astrology, and she likes to help people remember to be alive!

- Sam Moe is the recipient of a 2023 St. Joe Community Foundation Poetry Fellowship from *Longleaf Writers Conference*. Her work has appeared or is forthcoming from *Whale Road Review*, *The Indianapolis Review*, *Sundog Lit*, and others. Her poetry book *Heart Weeds* is out from Alien Buddha Press and her chapbook *Grief Birds* is forthcoming from *Bullshit Lit* in April '23. Her full-length *Cicatrizing the Daughters* is forthcoming from *FlowerSong Press*.

- Sara Wiser (she/her/hers) is a current Drama and Transcultural Literature student at The American University in Washington, DC. Originally from Philadelphia, Sara's work features musings on intimacy, love, loss, intergenerational trauma, sexuality, nature, and girlhood. Find more at www.SaraWiser.com or discover her on Instagram @sara.wiser

- Sarah Blakely is a poet and songwriter from California who primarily writes about relationships and sexual trauma. Her work has been published in anthologies by Sunday Mornings At The River, Papeachu Press, and Querencia Press. She also has self-published two poetry collections, *Volcano Girl*, and *The Fire Between Us*, available on Amazon and other online booksellers. Find her on Instagram at @sarahb.poetry

- Sarah Merrifield is a gay, non-binary, neurodivergent, and disabled poet who has been writing her entire life as a means to process pain and heal from trauma. Sarah uses she/they pronouns.

- Sarah is a poetry MFA candidate at Saint Mary's College of California where she works at the Center for Environmental Literacy. Sarah has been a writing coach and a teacher for ten years and enjoys writing ecopoetry, and inspiring young writers to express themselves through poetics. She lives in Oakland, CA with her husband and two kids.

- Scott Russell is 40 years old and lives in New Haven, Connecticut. Currently celebrating a decent 80% houseplant survival rate, they still don't get out enough, but have finally overcome all self-conscious hangups to go dancing at every opportunity. Discovering that all their unrealized software/art project ideas could be fed into a writer's world-building hopper (and still be fulfilling without having to actually code), Scott has their first piece of microfiction published in *Blood Tree Literature*, along with works shared on scotterussell.com.

- Shelley Sanders-Gregg (she/her) is a writer and poet, wife and mother of four from St. Louis, Mo. She holds a master's degree in social work and much of her poetry centers around hope and healing, nature, and the joys of motherhood. You can find more of her work on IG: @sgreggwrites

- Stephen Brown (he/him) is a Philadelphia-based writer, LGBT+ advocacy worker, and graduate student in literature with a passion for traditionally queer literary forms. His work has appeared in Wicked Gay Ways arts journal, Querencia Press, and others.

- Tara is a 24 year old poet living in London. She writes to explore the natural world and her place in it, and her experiences as a young woman trying to build her sense of self. She exists on instagram as @tara_d_poet and spends her time walking all over her city finding words to inspire the next poem.

- Theresa K. Jakobsen (they/them) is a German creative, who after spending the pandemic on the remote Faroe Islands re-entered the colorful streets of Berlin city. The special challenges of living in another country as a chronically ill person were a propulsion to their creativity. Theresa creates mixed media art, photography and writes multilingual pieces that circle around the theme of identity and relationships in a digital age. Their works recently got published in En*gendered Lit, Continue the Voice and Revolution Publication.

- Tori Louise grew up in a small mountain town in southern California, where she spent her childhood falling in love with the wonder of the natural world. Louise's writing is dipped in mysticism and adoration for the world, and an intense curiosity of the full spectrum of humanity. She is currently working on her first poetry collection and will be attending an Artist's residency at Chateau Orquevaux in the Winter of 2023. She currently resides in California, where she spends her days nestled in-between the mountains and the sea.

- Veronica S. is proud to be from a Native and Mexican American heritage, bringing the voices of her past into her work. She is originally from California but currently lives in Arizona where she continues to cultivate her writing. Veronica is an avid human rights advocate and you can often find her volunteering or helping any way she can.

- Veronica Szymankiewicz is a published poet from Miami, Florida. Her poetry varies quite a bit in genre and themes and is inspired directly from her own personal experiences, thoughts, and feelings. A lifelong writer and lover of words, she considers poetry to be a cathartic outlet. Veronica writes as a way to heal herself, with hopes that her words will resonate with others, healing them along the way as well.

- Victoria Johnson is 41 years old and has loved Photography since the age of nine. She is the owner of Skye Breese Photography, a small photography business in the Livingston, Texas area. She is from Independence, Louisiana and has roots in upstate New York as well. Victoria considers herself an all around photographer, enjoying several genres of photography. She is a monthly contributor to Native Hoop Magazine where her images of indigenous people have been published. She has several other publishments in her background as well. She has had two street images exhibited at a street photography showcase in San Antonio, Texas and one of her mobile photography images exhibited at a gallery at Lone Star College in Kingwood, Texas

- Violeta Garza (she/they/ella) is a Latinx poet, weaver, and performer from the Historic West Side of San Antonio, Texas. Their poems have been selected or are forthcoming in Acentos Review, Voices de la Luna, The Society for the Study of Gloria Anzaldúa, Samsara Magazine, and Arts Alive San Antonio. She has performed her original poems and stories for Texas Public Radio, The Alamo Chapter for Human Rights, The Curtain Up Cancer Foundation, and elsewhere. You can peruse their work at violetagarza.com or via Instagram at @violeta.poeta.

OTHER TITLES FROM QUERENCIA

Allison by Marisa Silva-Dunbar

GIRL. by Robin Williams

Retail Park by Samuel Millar

Every Poem a Potion, Every Song a Spell by Stephanie Parent

songs of the blood by Kate MacAlister

Love Me Louder by Tyler Hurula

God is a Woman by TJ McGowan

Learning to Float by Alyson Tait

Fever by Shilo Niziolek

Cutting Apples by Jomé Rain

Girl Bred from the 90s by Olivia Delgado

Wax by Padraig Hogan

When Memory Fades by Faye Alexandra Rose

The Wild Parrots of Marigny by Diane Elayne Dees

Hospital Issued Writing Notebook by Dan Flore III

Knees in the Garden by Christina D Rodriguez

Provocative is a Girl's Name by Mimi Flood

Bad Omens by Jessica Drake-Thomas

Beneath the Light by Laura Lewis-Waters

Ghost Hometowns by Giada Nizzoli

Dreamsoak by Will Russo

the abyss is staring back by nat raum

How Long Your Roots Have Grown by Sophia-Maria Nicolopoulos

CPSIA information can be obtained
at www.ICGtesting.com
Printed in the USA
BVHW021139210323
660854BV00010B/289